EXCEPTIONAL
ACCOMPLISHMENT

*Top Consultants, Trainers and Speakers
Share Winning Ideas So You Can Get More Done —
and Get More Out of Life!*

Compiled by Doug Smart

EXCEPTIONAL ACCOMPLISHMENT

Managing Editor: Gayle Smart
Editor: Sara Kahan
Proofing Editor: Laura Johnson
Book Designer: Paula Chance
Copyright ©2000

Disclaimer: This book is a compilation of ideas
from numerous experts who have each contributed a chapter.
As such, the views expressed in each chapter are those of the authors
and not necessarily the views of James & Brookfield Publishers.

For more information, contact:
James & Brookfield Publishers
P.O. Box 768024
Roswell, GA 30076
✆ 770-587-9784

Library of Congress Catalog Number 99-091921

ISBN: 0-9658893-8-6

10 9 8 7 6 5 4 3 2 1

All you need is the plan, the road map, and the courage to press on to your destination.

— Zig Ziglar

Every noble work is at first impossible.

— Thomas Caryle

CONTENTS

The E-T Factor:
How to Use
Entrepreneurial Thinking®
to Achieve Success in
Corporate America

by Jodi Walker

Corporate America is desperate to find new ways to adapt to the changing marketplace and stay on the cutting edge. But more important than that, slowly but surely companies have realized that they must have *people* in their organizations who think with a vision and are up to the challenge of breakthroughs, quality, and exceptional service. The E-T Factor is based on the concept of Entrepreneurial Thinking® and is a system designed to help individuals in corporate America accomplish more and exceed their own expectations. It is based on research that identifies key entrepreneurial success factors that can benefit everyone at all levels within an organization.

Many of America's largest and greatest corporations were founded by a single dedicated entrepreneur (IBM, Polaroid, Federal Express, Dell Computers). Individuals have been responsible for building large organizations, yet as the company grows, too often the talent within the workplace gets stifled. The challenge is to get individuals within an organization to utilize Entrepreneurial Thinking skills for the benefit of their own success as well as the success of the organization. It has to be a two-way street. For many, faith has to be restored to eliminate the

"Why am I working here?" syndrome. With the past and current trends of rightsizing and reorganizing, individuals oftentimes live in fear of what is coming next. This fear has caused many workers to strike out on their own.

But what about those who are still within the corporate environment, feeling the brunt of more work with fewer people and leaving work each day less than satisfied? How do we motivate them toward the corporate vision? The truth is we don't. They must learn to motivate themselves and create an entrepreneurial spirit for their own success and then be able to link it with the company vision and mission. In a survey conducted by the Gallup Organization of over 55,000 workers, there were several attitudes that correlated strongly with higher profits. One of those attitudes was that the individuals made a direct connection between their work and the company's mission.

The Entrepreneurial Thinking Factors are designed to assist organizations in developing their greatest resource — their PEOPLE! Allowing individuals to further develop their talent, utilize their creativity, think with a vision and still see the value of contributing to the team, makes ACCOMPLISHMENT inevitable.

Let's look at the **E-T Factors**:

Focused Vision

Accelerated Career Strategies

Confidence

Thinking Skills

Originality

Risk for Reward

Focused Vision

The entrepreneur is the visionary in all of us: The use of the imagination to spark the future of human advancements. Knowledge and expertise are not enough to keep pace with today's rapidly changing world. The high-pressure work environment is forcing people to take a closer look at the personal bottom line. In other words, ask yourself, "What does it take for me to be a peak performer in the workplace, and how far will I go for my company?" Today you must find new ways to stay focused, maintain energy, and relentlessly seek out ways to achieve your own personal mission and vision for your future.

For years individuals in corporate America were told, "Here is who we are and what we believe, and now here is how you need to think to be successful in this organization." The reality, of course, then led to a stifled environment that did not allow for future thinking.

In many of the workshops that I conduct across the country, I will ask the group, "Who can tell me what the corporate mission statement is?" Almost always, there are few, if any, hands up. Once a lady jumped up and said, "Wait a minute, I think I have it on a plaque on my wall." A gentleman said, "Didn't we get a coffee mug with the mission on it last year?" The bottom line is this: it doesn't matter if it is on the wall or on a coffee mug if it is not linked in the hearts and minds of the individuals. How can corporations expect individuals to take ownership for results if the individuals don't know where they fit into the corporate mission?

Over the last decade organizations have tried to improve productivity through reorganizing and re-engineering with little emphasis on individuals and the role they play in the future of the company. Many companies were left with low morale and flat productivity. The key is to allow individuals to define their personal bottom line, understand their personal mission, and then learn to link it with the company mission and vision. Leadership guru Warren Bennis states that in great groups the goals are in harmony: Each member seeks individual greatness while also supporting the group's mission. This is very similar to how a beautiful symphony brings together individual talent to create one harmonious sound.

When looking at your personal mission you may want to ask yourself the following questions:

- How do I want to contribute to the world?
- I feel best when I help people do what?
- I am most proud of my contribution to what?

I once asked an audience, "Have you ever been asked these questions before?" Only one lady raised her hand. She said that she had been asked similar questions at a CEO retreat. I thought how sad that her corporation thinks it is important enough to ask these questions only to the top executives. The real value comes from understanding individuals better at every level of the organization. As you begin to develop your personal mission, it will then be easier to see the links between your personal mission and that of your organization.

In defining your personal mission, take a look at your personal bottom line. The four keys to understanding your *personal bottom line:*

1. Analyze your strengths.
2. Prepare for your challenges.
3. Know what you are willing to give up.
4. Be the best you can be today.

There was a young man who worked in the shipping department of a company that made skateboards and snowboards. While he was on his break, he began doodling on a piece of paper. When his break was over, he got up and went back to his work area. A manager walked into the break room where the young man had been doodling. He asked, "Who did this?" He then went down to the shipping department to approach the young man, and he asked him, "Is this your doodling?" The young man reluctantly replied, "Well yes, but I was on my break." You see already the young man was prepared to hear something negative. The manager replied, "No that's not it at all; this doodling is really good. In fact, are you aware that down the hall we have a graphic arts department that puts this type of artwork on our skateboards and snowboards?" The rest is history. The young man now works in the graphic arts department. But, you see, it took someone else to help to identify those talents. It is essential to find ways to continually analyze and develop untapped potential, and it starts by being more aware of your strengths.

Once you better understand your strengths, it becomes easier to prepare for your challenges. As you develop your personal mission statement, it is important to know what, if anything, you are willing to give up in order to achieve the level of success you desire in your life. It is equally important to plan and set goals for your future that are in alignment with your personal mission. However, being the best you can be *today* sets your future in motion.

Accelerated Career Strategies

Entrepreneurs are notorious for getting the skills they need. "Being an educated person is no longer adequate," Peter Drucker explains in *Harvard Business Review*. Your current skills will not be enough to meet the challenges of tomorrow. It is obvious that you need to continually update your knowledge and skills. However, more important than that, you need to learn to create a focused state of mind that allows you to maintain energy and enthusiasm in order to be productive.

My father worked at the same company from the time he was 18 until he took early retirement 38 years later. This is almost unheard of today. The ideas of job security and status quo are completely outdated. Whether you are the CEO of a company or even if you own it, you don't have job security; businesses fail everyday. However, you do have job security if you prepare for lifetime employability. I am a firm believer that you make your own job security by always learning new skills, being open to new ideas, improving communication, and maintaining the "I Can" attitude. Unfortunately, the "That's not my job" attitude has filtered its way into many corporations.

Accelerated Career Strategies to propel your success:

1. Find a mentor for yourself and be willing to mentor others.

2. Learn how to team up for success. The team synergy can produce amazing results.

3. Learn to thrive on change. Entrepreneurial Thinkers know how to view change as a challenge.

4. Learn to be the "owner" of your job success. Take ownership for results!

5. Create excitement for life-long learning.

6. Begin by learning something new every single day.

"Continuous learning may be the only real source of sustainable competitive advantage for individuals in corporations today."

— Tom Peters

Confidence

What comes to mind when you hear the names Michael Jordan, Lee Iacocca, Bill Gates, Oprah Winfrey, Hallmark Cards, Kinko's, McDonalds or Starbucks? Do you immediately form some picture in your mind? Those individuals and companies stand out in a crowd. When you look at their successes and what they have accomplished, there is a common ingredient — Confidence. They have confidence in themselves, their ideas, and their companies.

Your confidence factor affects everything you do in life. The vision you create for yourself is useless if you don't have the confidence in yourself and your ability to fulfill your vision.

The Power of Five

There are five types of confidence that are key ingredients in the success formula.

- Inner Confidence
- Outer Confidence
- Communication Confidence
- Support System Confidence
- Bullet-proof Confidence

It is possible for people to display confidence outwardly but yet, deep down, be lacking inner confidence. However, what you believe about yourself on the inside is the key ingredient. *Inner confidence* and *outer confidence* must be congruent if you are to be viewed as authentic. If you don't truly believe in your ability to succeed, why would anyone else?

Communication confidence is important because people want to do business with people who know how to effectively convey their ideas to others.

Support System confidence means that you need to find one or more people who are supportive of your goals and dreams. Remember that sometimes even your friends and family can unintentionally try to squelch your dream by showing a lack of support. Share your ideas with those who share your enthusiasm.

Bullet-proof confidence is your ability to deal with dissension. I once heard a news broadcast that said, "A police officer has been shot but not injured." Then it dawned on me the only way to be shot and not injured is to be wearing a bulletproof vest. Bullet-proof confidence is your ability to bounce back. Entrepreneurs all over the world have successfully demonstrated the importance of bouncing back from failures. In corporate America it is just as important to be resilient and able to bounce back from failures or upsets in the work environment.

Thinking Skills

One of the chief sources of value today is knowledge and the ability to apply it in a timely manner. We are all aware that there are three types of people: Those that make it happen, those that watch it happen, and those that wonder what happened. Companies want individuals who know how to make it happen!

Jobs are becoming obsolete at a rate of 30-50% per year. Yet more often than not, you hear people talk about their fear of obsolescence instead of developing the thinking skills necessary to thrive in the future.

The brain is capable of more thought patterns than there are atoms in the universe. The Stanford Brain Institute says that the average person gets by on 2% of his or her mental potential. In essence, you are equipped with a high-tech computer without an instruction booklet. Brain scientists have found that intelligence is not fixed, and you become more intelligent based on the more you use and stimulate your brain.

Emotional Intelligence also plays a key role in our thinking skills and how we function. According to Daniel Goleman, author of the book *Emotional Intelligence*, "The science behind EQ, as it is often referred to, teaches us every day how to enhance our reasoning capacities and, at the same time, to make better use of the energy of our emotions, the wisdom of our intuition, and the power inherent in our ability to connect at a fundamental level with ourselves and those around us."

When you expand your thinking skills the results can be limitless.

Originality

The originality factor has repeatedly played a role in the success of individuals and organizations. Dell Computer Corporation grew to $1.7 billion in revenues in just ten years by defying the conventional wisdom that personal computers must be seen to be sold. A man named George de Mestral was brushing the burrs out of his wool pants and his dog's fur. He became curious about the burrs and looked at them under a microscope. The microscope revealed hundreds of tiny hooks that were snagged in bits of fur and wool. Years later, he invented Velcro®. Being curious and willing to be unconventional can stimulate creative and original ideas.

It has been said that there is an abundance of ideas in the marketplace. However, the skills to put the ideas into action and expand on the ideas through creativity are severely lacking. Creativity isn't a destination; it's a journey. Creativity and originality in business must be a way of life, a productive attitude developed by individuals throughout their business lifetimes, not a passing good idea that happens to work.

Enhancing Creativity and Originality

- Know your inner self.
- Slow down long enough to think.
- Create an environment for creativity to flourish.
- Pay attention to your thoughts.
- Destroy judgment .
- Ask new questions.
- Rely on your intuition.
- Broaden your perspective.

"To raise new questions, new possibilities, to regard old problems from a new angle, requires creative imagination."

— Albert Einstein

Risk

The final Entrepreneurial Thinking factor is risk. To take your creative ideas and your entrepreneurial strengths to a place where they can be recognized and utilized requires an element of risk: Moving out of the comfort zone and into an area all-too-often referred to as "off limits" in your mind. Although entrepreneurs are often considered risk takers, the research shows that they are "calculated risk takers." In other words, they are willing to be courageous and move out of the comfort zone, but they make well-thought-out, calculated decisions most of the time.

I once had an opportunity to interview Paul Orfalea, the founder of Kinko's. Paul is a great example of a visionary, someone willing to be unconventional and to take risks. He is someone who knows his strengths and challenges. Although he struggled with dyslexia, he knew his strengths were in finding opportunities and good people to work with him. Paul prided himself on referring to his employees as co-workers. He felt the term "employee " implied subordinate, and he wanted his co-workers to feel like valued members of the team. I used the word employees three times in the interview and he corrected me every time, proving he believed in his concept.

Paul started his copy business with one copier near a college campus, but he never stopped looking for opportunities. He started selling pens and pads that students might need on the first day of school. During the first few months of operation, he was selling over $2,000 a day in school supplies as well as selling copies. Kinko's now has over 1,000 locations worldwide. Paul describes an entrepreneur as a business person who exhibits both initiative and a high tolerance for risk. He also believes in instilling the entrepreneurial spirit in those who work with him.

In the corporate market in the past, and still today in many organizations, individuals have been scrutinized for taking risks that didn't result in positive results. However, some of the more progressive organizations actually embrace people for taking risks. They know that they can learn from failures and turn them into opportunities. Harvey Mackay, author of *Swim with the Sharks,* once said, "If you want to double your success ratio you have to double your failure rate." You have to be willing to step out of your comfort zone if you want to make a difference for yourself and your organization.

"There are risks and costs to a program of action.
But they are far less than the long-range risks and costs
of comfortable inaction."

— John F. Kennedy

ABOUT
JODI WALKER

*J*odi Walker is President of Success Alliances, a training and development company that works with individuals who want to take charge of
*their careers and organizations who want to develop their people potential.
Jodi is an award-winning internationally known speaker with a reputation
for high-energy presentations and getting the audience involved in the
learning process. Her focus is on getting individuals to tap into their true
potential in order to achieve personal and professional greatness.*

*In addition to Jodi's motivating keynotes, she trains in her areas of
expertise: customer service, communication, team building, dealing with
change, and the E-T Factor — Entrepreneurial Thinking.® Jodi works with
small and gigantic organizations and prides herself with delivering take-
home value that can be applied immediately. Jodi is also a singer and song-
writer who has written theme songs for business events.*

Contact Information:
Jodi Walker
Success Alliances
9018 Balboa Blvd., PMB #617
Northridge, CA 91325
phone: (800) 782-1719
fax: (818) 894-4329
e-mail: JodiWalker@aol.com
web: www.JodiWalker.com

CATCHING THE BALL:
SIX TECHNIQUES FOR JUGGLING
YOUR OVERLOADED LIFE

by Dan Thurmon

H ow's your juggling act? What objects, or should I say objectives, are you struggling to keep in the air? Let's see. There's your work, your family, your personal and professional growth, spiritual needs, friends, hobbies, and health, to name just a few. By the way, have you noticed that the pace of your activity and the demands for your time have increased exponentially in recent years? How many balls are you juggling right now? Are there too many? You are not alone.

As I work with corporations, associations, communities, and students throughout the country, I find a common sentiment: "We are going as fast as we can, and there's not enough time to accomplish everything!" People in today's competitive environment feel enormous pressure, both external and self-imposed, to do more, know more, make more, sleep less, and go faster. Never before have so many done so much and felt so unsatisfied.

This epidemic of activity reminds me of my childhood. At eleven years old I was frequently called "hyperactive." Maybe you've been there. Maybe your children are there now. I had so much energy inside my small body, and I had no idea how to express it to the world around me.

I would run amuck, expending energy in mass quantities on a dozen things at once. Nothing purposeful happened, but that didn't really matter. For me, the thrill of activity, the pace itself, was a rush. Activity spurred more activity, and it conveyed the illusion that I was getting something done. Have you ever felt this way? Can you remember times when the flurry of events, tasks, and people in your life have kept you busy but left you unfulfilled, wondering what was the point or purpose?

At school, my physical exuberance was seen as more than disruptive. It was unnatural. Teachers told my mother to try Ritalin. Fortunately, she decided against the drug, and about that time I discovered the first method of expression that completely captured my attention. I learned to juggle from an entertainer named Mike Vondruska at a Renaissance Festival in Bristol, Wisconsin. This was a turning point; my life would never be the same.

This physical and mental challenge intrigued me, and I loved it. I practiced relentlessly, putting in hours at a time. I was lost in the solitary activity of tossing objects above my head and around my body, then attempting to catch them with fluid coordination, maintaining the rhythmic flow of the juggling pattern. No longer an unfocused child, lacking "attention span," I could suddenly endure the tedious routine of attempting a trick hundreds of times without success. Sometimes, my hands were sore, tired, and cracked, but I would hardly notice. I was determined to persist until I would achieve one simple goal: the accomplishment of catching the ball.

Practice pays off. The techniques of expert juggling served me well as I developed entertainment skills, performing across the country and as far abroad as Saudi Arabia. I've used my talents to pay for college, work with celebrities, create job opportunities, and even meet the woman of my dreams, my wife Sheilia. Today, I am also a father, business owner, professional speaker, and entertainment producer. The applications and discipline of juggling have given new understanding to everything I have attempted since those early childhood years.

If you desire to improve your ability to accomplish more in your own life, it's time to get back to Juggling 101. We're talking about catching the ball. Making it happen. Getting results that matter. The techniques that work for world-class jugglers will work for you, as well. It takes practice, discipline, and determination, but the results are self-rewarding, and the challenge is fun. Let's get going.

1. Focus on Success — Looking Up

Whether you are learning to juggle three balls or seven, step one is to visualize the successful results of your efforts. It sounds simple, but you would be surprised how many frustrated beginners prefer to empty their hands, throwing the balls wildly in the hope that something positive will result. Frequently, when it doesn't work out the way they wanted, they'll try the same thing again, only faster.

Where do you place your focus? Focus is absolutely critical, which is why this chapter is called "Catching the Ball" instead of "Don't Drop the Ball!" Well-intentioned managers, teachers, and parents who lead others with expressions like "don't drop the ball" don't understand that they have just set up their employees, students, and children for failure and frustration. Before you begin a new challenge, whether it is a sales meeting, a conversation with a loved one, the creation of a business plan, or a five-ball pirouette, it is critical that you understand what success looks and feels like. Otherwise, how will you know when you achieve it?

One way to clarify your image of success with a particular skill is to watch others who are already accomplished and emulate their behavior. What do they do? What does it look like? What effect does it have? Place your focus on these images. Cement them into your brain and visualize the same results coming from your actions. For instance, if you would like to improve the way you communicate with others, think of someone you know who seems to have very effective communication skills. What does he or she do that makes a strong impression on you? Perhaps this person listens intently to others, maintaining eye contact and asking questions to clarify understanding. This seems to have a positive effect upon their relationships with others. They appear to be connected and engaged at a deeper, more meaningful level. Once you have observed and recognized this quality, you can envision yourself connecting with the people you encounter, taking the same actions in order to achieve similar results.

Successful jugglers always begin by looking up. In fact, the best jugglers continue to look up throughout the entire routine. By doing so, they are able to see the whole pattern. You have heard the expression "keep your eye on the ball." Well, this is NOT how it works. Try that, and you'll soon be staring at your hand, confirming the fact that you just caught one ball. Meanwhile, the rest of the balls are out of your view and instantly out of your control.

As leaders, you have many different balls in the air, responsibilities to coordinate, and tasks to accomplish day in and day out. The way to manage everything is to keep looking up. That is, you must have a clear focus on where you want your throws to go, and then execute each action with the best of your talents toward those goals. Keep looking up, and you'll develop an ability to view the entire pattern. Then, the catches begin to happen with much greater frequency.

2. Where Do I Start? — Prioritizing

What is the single most important thing you are doing today? Can you answer that question? If not, you will likely find it difficult to feel productive or purposeful as you conduct your daily juggling act. An optimum performance starts with a plan, and the first step in planning is to honestly assess your priorities.

There is a certain sequence that must occur in practice. When I teach beginning juggling, I'll typically spend several minutes teaching with one ball, clarifying the components of a perfect throw. Anxious and eager students will almost always become bored with this exercise, rushing to grab the other two balls and get to the real deal. But without taking the time to master the fundamentals, it becomes much more difficult to move forward and achieve the end result we desire.

Once you have clarified your focus (the vision you have for success), you need to determine the intermediate steps toward achieving that goal. What must happen in order for you to master the skills or achieve the objectives you desire? Be honest and exhaustive in your list, and then create a plan, or a sequence of steps, that will build your momentum. The first steps should provide you with the knowledge and skills to serve as a foundation. By sequencing and prioritizing your learning process this way, you will also manifest enthusiasm and experience the thrill of achieving small successes along the way.

I have found it extremely useful to utilize a daily planner each morning. Before I get into my productive mode, I spend a few minutes planning successful outcomes. The use of a good day planner may introduce the discipline needed to define top priorities of the day, week, and month. These priorities are ever-changing, so the habit of daily planning will help you stay on track.

Without clearly defined priorities, it is easy to become paralyzed when confronted with an overwhelming workload. We are defeated before we begin by the question, "Where do I start?" By being able to refer to your priorities, you'll be able to step back to a strategic perspective and refocus your energy. Of course, once you know that answer to the question, "What is the most important thing you have to do today?," it's up to you to follow through!

3. One Throw at a Time — Synthesis

Juggling is often misunderstood as the skill of doing many different things all at the same time. It looks that way, especially when performed by an expert. But, as one who has spent the majority of his life studying the art and science of juggling, I can tell you that this is an incorrect assumption. Juggling is not about doing many things at once. It is about doing one thing at a time, really, really fast.

Attempt to do many things at once, and you will fragment your focus. You'll also make yourself crazy. But if we do just one thing at a time, with concentrated focus, we can execute each throw to the best of our ability, then move on to the next with all of our attention and talent. The first throw may still be airborne, but once we've done our part, making the most accurate throw possible, it is out of our control. Our energy is misspent if we continue to worry about what is happening with that ball until, of course, it returns to our pattern in sequence. Then, when it requires more input and action, we will give the matter our complete focus once again.

Sounds easy, right? It's true that when we are most effective and our efforts are providing the greatest possible value, we are not doing many things at once, but one thing at a time, thoughtfully, quickly, and accurately. It is a true discipline to be "compartmentalized" with our thoughts and actions. The skill of being "in the moment," one hundred percent focused on the person you're with or your top priority project, separates those who struggle from those who lead.

So, which ball do you focus on? The answer: the one in your hand. If the ball is in your hand, throw it! The moment you have an idea or a new opportunity presents itself is usually the best time to take action. Go ahead and make a throw. Write down the idea. Put your plan in motion, taking the next step toward achieving your goal. When you have enough information to move a project forward, follow through on your thoughts and do it right then. This way, you will build momentum and develop a sense of rhythm with your actions.

I know what you are thinking. "This sounds really good, Dan, but it's not very realistic. I wish I could just do one thing at a time, but other people keep throwing balls at me! There isn't enough time in the day to do one thing at a time and get it all done!" You are absolutely correct. In today's fast-paced, competitive environment, there is another skill you must add to your repertoire: the ability to synthesize.

A synthesis is defined as "the combination of separate parts or elements in order to form a whole." Any time we attempt to execute two tasks simultaneously, the end result is a new, synthesized creation, and it is different from either of the other two. This is an important point, and it was driven home for me the first time I ever tried juggling while riding a unicycle. I thought it would be no problem. I had been juggling for a few months, and I had also just learned how to unicycle. So, juggling on top of the unicycle seemed like a reasonable next step. I mounted the one-wheeled contraption, three balls in hand. I threw the first, the second, and maybe the third. I don't really know. You see, as I was watching the two balls fly through the air, for just a split second I forgot I was riding a unicycle. That's all it took, and I hit the ground hard. I realized that the new challenge was much more difficult than either of the two tasks individually. It was a completely different skill, and it would certainly take practice.

Do you remember the first time you ever tried driving a car while placing a call on your cell phone? Thought it would be easy, didn't you? After all, you had many years of experience with both driving and making phone calls. But the moment you started steering with your knee, negotiating traffic and searching for those tiny buttons, you realized this task was completely new to you. The reason is, it was a synthesis. You weren't doing two things at the same time, driving your car *and* dialing a cell phone. Instead, you were still doing one thing at a time. But now it was a new, synthesized task called "driving your car *while* dialing a cell phone." Do you see the difference? Just as with the unicycle, it took practice and repetition to achieve the measure of comfort and safety that, I hope, you possess today.

Every time we attempt to synthesize two tasks, we really create a challenging third, and it takes practice to get it right. The same phenomenon takes place when you carry on a phone conversation *while* typing on your computer, or when you seek to improve service to your customer *while* managing profitability, or when you take on additional responsibilities *while* continuing to do the rest of your job. Keep this concept in mind as you exercise creativity every day, and have fun learning and mastering each new creation.

4. Mastering New Challenges — Find the Similarities

When I was twelve I pleaded with my mother until she finally consented to let me juggle fire torches. I was excited. I was thrilled. I was also more than a little bit scared. After all, nothing I had experienced with my juggling thus far could quite prepare me for the sensation of blazing fire flying inches from my head and body. You could say I reached a "psychological barrier."

I approached my mentor, Mike, and he understood my dilemma. He had also been through the "trial by fire," and knew that, until you light the torches and begin, you can't really understand what it's all about. What he told me, however, eased my concerns and provided me a system for handling this and other daunting challenges. Mike said, "Juggling fire is very similar to juggling clubs. In fact, it's exactly the same pattern, the same flip of the object. Just don't catch the wrong end." Easy for him to say. But he was right. I had been juggling clubs for a while, and I was pretty good at that. Aside from the fire, it was the same. In fact, following his advice, I practiced with my unlit torches to get used to the feel, the weight and the balance before adding the fuel and flame.

By the time I was ready to try it for real, I had developed a measure of confidence that was based not on my ability to juggle torches, but on my competence with the preparatory skills that are very *similar* to juggling torches. With that in mind, it was simply a leap of faith to follow through and embrace the new experience. I'm happy to say that I completed the task without setting fire to the house, the yard, the dog, or myself. Since that day, I have used the same method of associating the similarity of what I already knew to attempt and to succeed at challenges such as juggling knives, battle axes, and flaming machetes, as well as riding fifteen-foot-tall unicycles and doing backward double flips in a tumbling routine.

To excel and improve at what you do, you must take risks. You need to act outside your comfort zone. But venturing into unfamiliar territory can be a stressful undertaking. If you happen to feel anxious, apprehensive, or fearful about the things that are new to you, ask yourself, "What about this is similar to something I've done before?" Immediately, you will be able to draw comparisons to previous experiences you've had and to skills you have practiced throughout your life.

This is the same reason professional negotiators "role play" their assignments in order to prepare for upcoming engagements. A potential adversary, usually played by one of their peers, will throw every conceivable objection on the table, offering challenge after challenge to overcome. Having completed such an intensive rehearsal, any one of us would be confident and prepared to take the next step.

Asking yourself to determine what is similar about the new event has another positive result. At the same time, this exercise will help you to determine exactly what is different. Perhaps it is a new application of a familiar concept. Or, maybe the situation you are undertaking requires additional knowledge about a specific area of your job. Whatever the case, by isolating the components needing improvement, you will know where your new priorities reside, and you can get to work without wasted motion.

The reality is you can only begin to improve from where you are at this moment. We are all a sum total of our lifelong experiences, education, and relationships. And the skills that brought you here, to where you are and what you are doing right now, are the same skills you will need to apply in order to go further down the road to success. We constantly shape our personality and capabilities by choosing what we add to our repertoire and by using what we already possess. By associating the similarities and embracing the differences, you will develop confidence and enthusiasm that will help you accomplish more. You will also begin to captivate and inspire those around you.

5. Maintaining Control — Create a Pattern for your Life

In the world of juggling, one of the benchmarks that separates those who fool around from those serious about their craft is the challenge of juggling five balls. I have worked extremely hard at that task. I've spent countless hours and dropped thousands of times in order to eventually attain that accomplishment. There is a secret to success, and I am happy to share the secret with you.

In order to manage the increased pace, of course, your throws have to be more precise. Each toss must hit the mark, because you don't have time to compensate for errors. But struggling to attain "perfect throws" is extremely frustrating and disconcerting. I didn't learn five balls until I stopped focusing on each throw and began to focus on the pattern that was created by the five objects as they moved together in harmony. Then, I was able to relax and surrender to the pattern, the system for success, and the throws naturally became more consistent. In order to catch the next ball, the one after that, and all the balls that follow, you must have a solid pattern.

What's your pattern, your system for success? The main difference between the person who is an effective juggler and the one who is being effectively juggled is control. You must be in control. You are the one who has the final authority as to the content of your life's experience. You are the "pilot in command," to use an aviation term. So, are you flying the plane, or are you currently on automatic pilot?

It's up to you to carefully select the relationships, career goals, personal goals, spiritual goals and recreational pursuits that really matter to you. What is it that defines your uniqueness? These answers are critical to your happiness and how you will experience life. For that reason, it is essential that you are honest and thorough. Write it down. List everything you dream of doing, everything you are doing now, the things you enjoy and everything that is driving you nuts. Once this information is in front of you on paper, you can begin to organize your ideal pattern.

How do the objectives fit together? Do they support one another in such a way that success in one area will fuel success for the entire pattern? Or, are some of the "balls" in conflict, headed for a collision course somewhere in your future? What do you need to remove from the pattern in order to make your life more congruent and free of obstacles that are blocking you? If you feel today's challenge is already too intense, that your capacity is being pushed to its limit, and still you are trying to add something more, you must consider removing something from your pattern first!

Understand that this is only a snapshot of your life. The pattern continues to change moment to moment. Nothing is ever completely in its place, organized in a way that will finally make you content and peaceful. We can only seek to find peace and contentment in the *process* of juggling. There is only a beginning to our expertise, our skills and our accomplishments. There is no end. The pattern is always changing. As

Oscar Wilde wrote, "The systems that fail are those that rely on the permanency of human nature and not its growth and development."

6. Embracing the Challenge — Increase Self Expectations

When I was eleven and finally felt the satisfaction of juggling three balls, I instantly asked myself, "How do you do four?" So I tried it and had no success whatsoever. My mentor taught me that there was a different pattern for four, a different system that allowed it to work. He taught me the pattern, and I really understood it. Then I tried it and, with practice, began to realize success.

But as I kept practicing four balls, I started to notice something quite interesting: my three-ball juggling was getting really good. And the truth is, I didn't get the hang of four until I tried five. I am talking about increasing your own self-expectations. People ask me if I can do six, and I tell them yes, because I am working on seven. But my seven-ball juggling is a real struggle. I can just start to see the pattern, then, after a dozen throws or so, I drop a ball . . . or several. Maybe that's because I haven't tried eight.

If you think what you are doing now is difficult, I'd like to encourage you to try the next hardest thing. When you do, the challenges you face today will become easier to handle. As you continue to push the limits of your abilities, you will develop confidence and enthusiasm that enables you to succeed and inspires those around you.

You have the potential to be a world-class performer and expert juggler. All it takes is action and the commitment to incorporate these disciplines into your life: Raise your sights, prioritize, synthesize, associate the similarities of previous successes, and focus on the entire pattern that is the sum of all you do. One throw at a time, you will begin to have much greater success with the accomplishment of "catching the ball."

ABOUT
DAN THURMON

*D*an Thurmon *is a dynamic speaker who blends powerful messages in a unique style he terms "Speaking with Visual Impact." His clients include such diverse organizations as IBM, Coca-Cola, Delta Airlines, AT&T, Kimberly Clark Corporation and Aramco Oil in Saudi Arabia. Through active audience involvement, clever demonstrations and clear, concise advice for higher achievement, Dan makes real the power of taking action. His expertise is in helping people manage seemingly unmanageable workloads. A 1990 graduate of the University of Georgia, Dan and his family reside in Atlanta.*

Contact Information:
Dan Thurmon
InfoMedia, Inc.
4805 Lawrenceville Hwy., Suite 116
Lilburn, GA 30047
phone: (770) 923-3788
e-mail: Dan@DanThurmon.com

THE M.A.G.I.C.
OF ACCOMPLISHMENT

by Myra McElhaney

A s a young girl I wanted to be a beautiful princess whose heart was won by a charming prince who swept her away to live happily ever after. Did you? Guys, did you want to be the prince on the white horse that slew the dragon, saved the village, and won the heart of the princess?

My favorite fairy tale was Cinderella. There she was, working hard, making the best of her situation, and not bothering anyone. Then her fairy godmother appeared, waved her magic wand, and suddenly Cinderella was ready for the ball.

Her ragged clothes became a beautiful designer gown. Her stringy hair was suddenly a shiny, bouncy, fashionable coiffure. (That's a fancy word that means hair-do.) The smell of cinder-ash was replaced with the sweet fragrance of a fine perfume. The fairy godmother turned a pumpkin into an imported, luxury carriage. With another wave of her magic wand, common field mice became handsome, well-dressed men. Then, the biggest miracle of all, tiny little glass slippers *so* comfortable you could dance all night. *No pinched toes! No bunion pain!* Yes!

Well, I grew up in the 70's when record numbers of women were entering the workforce. We were taught that we could have it all: A happy family, a successful career, big money. We could scale the corporate ladder with grace and agility.

I knew that Prince Charming was not the answer for me. I began to believe in *The Career Fairy*. You know — if you get a job with a good company, be on time, do your work, don't cause any trouble — the Career Fairy will wave her magic wand and zap you with promotions, a six-figure income, and recognition for a job well done.

Have you seen the Career Fairy? I've been in the workforce for almost 25 years now and I've seen no sign of her skinny little butt. (Hey, if you could grant wishes wouldn't you have a skinny little butt?)

Now I have met some wicked witches. I have eaten some poison apples. I've fought a fire-breathing dragon or two. I've even encountered a few charming princes. And lots of frogs. But the Career Fairy — now THAT is make believe.

Just like *you*, I have found that companies aren't gingerbread houses. Most wicked witches are just gals trying to do their job. Slaying dragons isn't as easy as it looks. And the Career Fairy *ain't gonna show*. But you know, you don't have to ask the wizard for a brain. You don't even need a magic wand. Within each of us is all the M.A.G.I.C. we need to zap ourselves with personal accomplishment.

You have the M.A.G.I.C. within you.

M is for Mission

Several years ago I had a co-worker and friend named Browny Stephens who was dying of cancer. When I visited his hospital room he would often begin to reminisce about things we'd done in the past. He'd say, "Remember the first white-water rafting trip we all went on together?"

"Hey, what about the time we went hiking and y'all got caught in the ice storm on the way back?" Sitting in that hospital room we would retell and relive the stories of past adventures. I was a little uneasy about this because I was afraid it would make him sad knowing that he would never have experiences like that again.

The director of the hospital was also a friend of his. She told me that as people are dying they like to talk about things they have done in their lives and places they've been. It helps to validate that their life — *did* matter. That they *lived.* That they *made a difference.*

Steven Covey, author of *Seven Habits Of Highly Successful People,* says, "Start with the end in mind." When I think of visiting Browny in the hospital during those last weeks, I realize that we should *live* with the end in mind. Aware of what we want to look back on. Aware of the memories we're making. Aware of how we want to be remembered. Aware that we make those choices every day.

I never heard Browny talk of a mission or a purpose for his life, but when I think of Browny I think of the way he approached life — with a spirit of adventure and fun. No, he wasn't *always* hiking, rafting and dancing, but he had a way of looking at even everyday things as an adventure. And he made life an adventure for those around him. When I think of Browny, I don't see him lying in the hospital bed. I can see him at Octoberfest, wearing a paper mustache and dancing the "Funky Chicken"!

As I started my business of speaking and training, I knew that a business needed a mission statement. So I set out to develop a concise statement of the overall goal of my business.

Since motivating people through sharing my personal stories and life lessons is very personal, I realized that what I really needed was a mission statement for my *life.* A statement that sums up what I believe to be my purpose on earth. What I would like people to remember after I'm gone.

Now maybe it doesn't sound too business-minded, but I just didn't feel compelled to live a life that ended with a group of customers surrounding my casket weeping as they discussed how much I'd affected their bottom line. I thought it should be something more. Something profound.

Have you tried this? It was more difficult than I anticipated. I looked inward, outward, upside down, and backward to figure out my life's meaning.

My husband is in sales. His territory is the state of Georgia. When my schedule permits, I sometimes travel with him. One week he was visiting customers in Savannah, and we were staying in nearby Tybee Island. That day I was pensive and contemplating my purpose in life, trying to figure out my mission. As we walked on the beach that evening, I asked him, "Phil, do you ever wonder why we're here?" He quickly responded, "Because I have to cover the state of Georgia."

His quick, dry wit lightened up the moment for us both. In reflection I realized how often in my life I've gotten so involved in the day-to-day task of *doing* that I've lost the focus of *being*. Being on-target with what we want our lives to *be* gives meaning and purpose to what we *do*.

A few weeks later I answered the phone to hear the voice of Ken, a business associate and mentor. I asked, "How are you today?" He answered with his usual, "Doing great!" Then quickly retracted, "No, actually I'm not having such a great day today. That's why when I picked up my phone messages, yours went straight to the top. I knew after I talked to you I'd feel better!"

I don't remember the rest of our conversation, but after hanging up the phone his words echoed in my ear. "I knew after I talked to you I'd feel better!" What a compliment! It brought to mind the words, written months earlier, by an anonymous participant in one of my classes. She wrote, "Myra makes you feel better about being who you are."

Suddenly it clicked. I'd been looking for some grand, profound mission and here it was, given to me in simplicity. Make people feel better. I wanted my life to be significant. I wanted to change the world. Now I realize that if I can in some way make one person feel better, then that person is able to do better work, have better relationships, live more fully.

If I live with a focus on positively influencing each person I meet,

I can positively influence the world — one person at a time.

As a speaker, trainer, author and person, it is my mission to help people laugh, learn, and like themselves better.

Do I always make each and every person I encounter feel better? Afraid not. I am human. But if I can keep that focus and hold on to that aspiration many others feel better and I become a better person in the process.

M is for Mission. Your mission doesn't have to be profound or intellectual. Simply decide what you want to be remembered for and get busy creating it.

A is for Anchor

Faith Popcorn, chairman of the BrainReserve, is author of *The Popcorn Report* and *Clicking*. She studies trends and advises major corporations on how to capitalize on the shifts in consumer purchasing habits. She identifies a growing trend of spiritual exploration. Popcorn says that we are looking for ways to ground ourselves by learning from the past to prepare for the future. She calls this trend "anchoring."

For many people there is a return to their faith. Church attendance is showing record numbers. Books on religion, spirituality, and prayer are showing up on the bestseller list with regularity.

Newspapers are devoting entire sections to religion and inspiration. Television shows and movies are featuring angels and miracles. Disney's "Prince of Egypt" is a blockbuster children's movie.

Reportedly, more than 30 medical schools now offer courses in spirituality. They've proven that praying and having faith in spiritual beliefs help people to heal more quickly.

Whether it's that old-time religion or a "new age" concept, we are again looking to our core beliefs to define and guide us. We are remembering and reexamining our principles and our philosophies. We're identifying the source of our inspiration and looking for inner peace and serenity. We want to feel grounded. We're looking for an anchor.

As I was reading about this trend, its evidence and its effect on society, I was subconsciously fingering the charm bracelet I was wearing. As I looked down I was holding a little charm that symbolizes faith, hope, and charity. It is a cross, a heart, and an anchor. The anchor is a symbol of hope. Hope is faith, a desire accompanied by expectation of fulfillment.

Larry King, host of CNN's *"Larry King Live"* has a new book called *Powerful Prayers*. Although he describes himself as an agnostic, he was encouraged by his daughter to ask the many powerful people he interviews about their views on prayer.

Mr. King interviewed religious leaders, government leaders, athletes, and entertainers. He talked with Jews, Muslims, Buddhists, Baptists, Catholics, Mormons, New Age gurus, and people who professed no religion at all.

Interestingly, many of their thoughts and comments on prayer were similar: That prayer was just as beneficial, if not more so, to the person praying than the thing being prayed about, regardless of whom was being prayed to. Most said that prayer helped them to stay centered and grounded. Even many of the people who said they don't believe in a "god" admitted that they pray.

Many people find a spiritual connection when they attend a church, temple, or synagogue. Others connect most easily when they're in nature: A walk in the woods or sitting in a garden. I find that when I'm in the mountains, whether it's driving through the Blue Ridge Parkway or visiting the Grand Tetons, the words to "How Great Thou Art" often come to mind as I enjoy the beauty and splendor.

A few years ago I began keeping a "gratitude journal," a special book to list things I'm grateful for each day. The most interesting thing happened. I began to *look* for things to list in my journal. This made me more aware of the simple pleasures in my life. Like the warmth of a cup of coffee in my hands. Seeing my daddy smile. The smell of fresh air the first spring day it's warm enough to open the windows. Sunday afternoon motorcycle rides with my husband. Giving thanks is one way to connect spiritually.

An additional benefit was that on days I don't feel so grateful I can flip through my journal and remember some things that bring a smile to my face.

I, like many others, also use prayer, meditation, and affirmations to stay spiritually connected. Many people find that doing something creative or artistic, reading inspirational poems or books, or playing a musical instrument helps them to feel anchored or grounded.

How do you connect with your spirit, with God, or your "higher power?" How do you "ground" yourself? What is your anchor?

A is for anchor. Being in touch with our spirit helps us to take comfort in being part of the bigger picture. It helps us keep a healthy perspective. It helps us to rise above the daily grind and focus on our purpose. Schedule time for nurturing your inner spirit.

G is for Gang

One day I was watching a TV talk show about gangs. Now I'm not someone who lies around watching talk shows all day. No, really. I only watch them for research. That's right, research. You never know where that great story or idea will come from. It's research, I tell you.

Anyway, on this show Geraldo was interviewing gang members. He asked the question, "Why do you want to be part of a gang?" Their answers amazed me.

This young urban street kid who had admitted to robberies and beatings said a gang gave him a *sense of belonging*. He was proud to wear their colors and let others know he was part of that gang.

The gang had rules. He said that everyone knew what was expected of him or her and what the consequences would be if these expectations weren't met.

The gang gave him protection. He said, "I know if anything happens my 'homeboys' will take care of me."

As human beings we all have common needs. The need to belong, to understand the rules, to feel safe, had driven these kids to become associated with a negative group that was bound together in crime, violence, and antisocial behavior.

These same needs prompt us to act positively and become part of teams, fraternities, civic clubs, and support groups.

I think the word "gang" has gotten a bad rap. We've come to associate it only with a band of antisocial adolescents when there are other, more positive meanings. According to *Webster's Dictionary*, "gang" can also mean "a group of persons working together" or "a group of persons having informal and usually close personal relations."

We all need a gang. Operating in an arena where we "know the rules" helps us to feel secure and stable. Knowing that our "home boys," our confidants, our comrades, will take care of us gives us comfort. When we surround ourselves with people who believe in us, people with common goals and values, people who support our ideas, our growth is nurtured and we are able to accomplish more.

G is for gang. Let's create a gang or support system whose colors we'd be proud to wear.

I is for Initiative

My mother worked for many years in a cotton mill. She worked in the "Card Room" (they called the departments "rooms.") This is the first department cotton is sent to as it begins the process of being carded, combed, spun, and woven into fabric.

After several years of operating the various machines in this department, the "Fixer" job came open. The "Fixer" performed maintenance services on the machines and "fixed" them when they weren't working properly.

Mama approached her boss and told him she would like to be considered for the "Fixer" job. He promptly told her that he couldn't put her in that job because they'd never had a female "Fixer" before. He went on to explain how physically demanding the job was.

Undaunted, she pointed out that *all* the jobs in that department were physically demanding. She said, "I've operated every machine in this department. I've worked here longer than anyone in this department. I deserve this promotion." She went on to make him a proposition. She promised, "Give me this job for one year, and, if at the end of that year you don't feel I'm doing as good a job as any male Fixer you've ever had, I'll step down." He reluctantly agreed.

Mama went to town and bought herself a big, bright red toolbox to carry her tools to work in. She was the Fixer in the Card Room for two years before being promoted to the Industrial Engineering Department.

Initiative: the ability and aptitude to make introductory steps and initiate action. Mama had it. She didn't wait for someone else to make the first move. She didn't let ". . . it's never been done before" stop her.

I is for initiative. Being willing and able to get going and keep going, even if it's tough, is crucial for accomplishment.

C is for Commitment

When Phil and I married, I began joining him on his annual ski trip with friends. This trip was a well-established tradition.

Phil is a natural athlete. I'm not. In addition to not liking cold weather, I had memories of being the proverbial "last chosen" for teams in school P. E. activities and being laughed off the court in my only tennis lesson. I guess you could say I'm athletically challenged. Something to do with eye-hand coordination, I'm told — or maybe coordination in general. However, being eager to please my new husband and looking forward to a new adventure, I committed to give it a try.

The first year I assured Phil that he should go on to ski the "black" slopes with his friends and not to worry about me. I would sign up for a beginner lesson and give it a try. Now I know some couples would have thought it fun and romantic for the husband to teach the wife to ski. I didn't marry until my mid-thirties; I had seen some reality. I figured it would be better for our marriage if he went on to enjoy the sport with his friends while I fell, cursed, and made a fool of myself in front of total strangers.

(Especially since when I asked Phil how he learned to ski, he told me his friend rode the lift with him to the top of a mountain and told him to point his skis downhill and go. I figured I'd need a little more instruction than that!)

The beginner class was right where I belonged. It started with, "This is a ski." "This is a pole." That part I got; my confidence was building. The young, cute girl who was our instructor told us she usually teaches children. I felt reassured. She demonstrated using the pole to knock the snow off your ski boot, putting on your skis, and taking off your skis. Then we put on one ski and walked around in a circle. I was a little shaky, but I could do this. She then demonstrated "duck walking" up hill. Well, you couldn't call it a hill, really. She instructed us in making a "pie." That's making a wedge with your skis to move slowly. (That's the theory anyway.)

Eventually we worked up to the rope pull. This I liked. We stood in line and held onto a rope that pulled us up a tiny little hill. Probably a two percent incline. (For you treadmill users, that's the first notch on your incline adjustment.) We would then zoom down the "hill" at lightning speed. Well, it seemed that way to me. Some of the others in the class were eager to attack the first real lift. Show-offs! I was happy to continue working right there on that little hill. But noooooo! Off we go to the lift.

My friend Connie had told me that, for her, the lift was the scariest part because if you weren't careful, you would fall getting off the lift, and you had to get out of the way quickly because others were getting off the lift behind you. I listened intently to the instructions about how to position yourself to push off the seat and safely exit the lift.

Gosh, there was so much to remember. Slide forward on the seat, hold poles together in inside hand so they don't get caught on the chair. With the poles in that hand, place your fist down on the seat, other hand on the "arm" of the seat, feet straight, push and lift. And I was off! Victory! Accomplishment! I'd made it off the lift.

Now I looked down the mountain. OH, MY GOD!!!!! There are people everywhere! The instructor is yelling to make a pie. It's straight down! Think, think, shins forward, make a pie, turn.

I won't give you all the gory details. Let's just say that somewhere about half-way down I told the nice man who had repeatedly helped me get up that I appreciated his kindness and help, but if he would just get those things off my feet I would walk down that mountain.

I failed the beginner ski class.

Another day. Another beginner class. This instructor was some hot-shot young guy who obviously learned to ski as an infant and was just an instructor to fill the time between flirting with girls and dare-devil skiing. Can you believe he had the audacity to yell at me??? I don't think he understood that I was his customer. I was appalled at his lack of rapport-building skills. I was *paying* for this torment. I deserved to be treated with some respect. I vowed that if I lived to get off that mountain I'd report his rude behavior.

Day three: Shopping. Now here's a sport where I excel.

The next year I decided to give it another try. Ski trips can be dull if you don't ski. Anyway, there was another girl in our group that year who was a beginner, too. I should at least make an effort.

Beginner Class #3: The instructor was a boney, leather-skinned fellow about 50 years old. A former competitive skier, he was now instructing. He moved so naturally on skis they seemed a part of him.

As we stood facing him I was prepared to hear, "This is a ski." (That part I retained from my two previous beginner lessons.) Instead he looked slowly over the group, giving eye contact to each individual.

"The first thing I want you to do today is to decide why you are here. Are you here because someone else wants you to be here? Did you feel obligated to come? Or, are *you* here because you *want* to learn to ski?"

In that moment I decided that *I* wanted to learn to ski. That was it. I was going to learn to ski because *I — wanted — to — ski*. Before, I had just planned to take a lesson. This time I committed to learning to ski.

At the end of that lesson I was zooming down the bunny slope. I was a maniac. I met Phil and the others at lunch with the excitement of a first grader. "Watch me ski! Watch me ski! I can do it!"

After lunch Phil (who skis the feared "black diamond" slopes) accompanied me to the bunny slope and saw an adult woman with knees bent, shins forward, in a deep wedge tentatively maneuver her way down a hill. What I felt was the wind in my face, snow spraying as I turned, the thrill of victory!

It may sound overly simplistic, but a major step in accomplishment is the commitment: Setting your goal and deciding that this is something you will do. In other areas of my life as in skiing, I've found that once I make that commitment, I won't settle for anything less.

Also, do it on your own terms. Your accomplishment may not look like someone else's. No one else is skiing in your boots. The crowd doesn't have to point and gasp, "Look at her go!" for you to feel the wind in your face and the thrill of victory.

C is for Commitment. Commit to the accomplishment you desire.

Mission, Anchor, Gang, Initiative, Commitment.
You have the M.A.G.I.C. to accomplish your own happy endings.

ABOUT
MYRA MCELHANEY

*M*yra McElhaney works with organizations that want to build stronger customer loyalty through higher employee satisfaction. Through keynotes, workshops and development of educational resources, Myra connects. She has fifteen years experience in sales and customer contact in various industries, including fashion, retail, real estate, and advertising. She has been a professional speaker and trainer for nine years. Her quick wit, warm style and use of real life examples make her learning sessions fun, memorable and implementable. Myra is the author of "Mama Always Says. . ." and co-author of "Reach for the Stars".

Contact Information:
Myra McElhaney
McElhaney & Assoc.
8531 Birch Hollow Drive
Roswell, GA 30076
phone: (770) 664-4553
fax: (770) 752-0817
e-mail: MyraMcElhaney@mindspring.com
web: speakerspages.com/MyraMcElhaney

GET MORE ACCOMPLISHED AND HAVE MORE FUN — WITH THE PROACTIVE DECISION-MAKING PROCESS

by Deborah L. Dahm

At the end of 1998 a dental practice wanted to evaluate the successes and obstacles of the past year. They wanted to move into the next year with new and fresh directions. They focused their decision-making on what had been done wrong and what should have been done better. Through all this negative thinking, they were subtracting from their experiences. They had literally started the process in the "red," a negative balance. Why not rethink this process, starting the process in the "black" with a positive balance by thinking about successes? Couldn't they take those successes to new levels of accomplishments?

In my work as a trainer, consultant, and author I have never lost sight of the wisdom of the Enneagram, a personality typology, that addresses the internal motivation of personality. Understanding the internal motivation behind external behavior has enhanced my ability to communicate and work with others more effectively. So how does this relate to decision-making? As a facilitator for many organizations I have been able to take people of all levels of management through the

Proactive Decision-Making Process. This process creates an environment that solves problems or takes a successful adventure to the next level. All businesses share many of the same challenges: stress, increased competition, changes in technology, human resource challenges, and administrative challenges.

In a proactive work environment people automatically become more open, creative, and flexible in their thinking. They are willing to take the risk of stating their opinions. They actually have fun. Did I say "fun"? Yes. When we allow people and ourselves to have fun, we create a place where people are excited and look forward to coming to work each day.

When organizations involve every person on a team in a Proactive Decision-Making Process, success results on three levels: success for the employee, success for the team, and, ultimately, success for the organization. The benefits and successes for employees who are made part of the Proactive Decision-Making Process include empowerment, enthusiasm, motivation, and emotional buy-in to the decision. The more people feel that they are part of a process, the more invested they become in that process and its implementation.

Once individuals feel success, they contribute to the success of the team. Everyone comes to the table with heightened awareness of each other's strengths and challenges. The third level of success is dependent upon employee and team success: organizational success. Although many leaders realize this idea intellectually, seldom are employees truly involved in the decision-making process. When an organization implements the Proactive Decision-Making Process, it realizes more than success. It sees proactive change. When the employees and the teams are implementing their own ideas, the benefits of change become evident to all.

Step #1 — Sharing the Success

Each of us has specific perceptions of what success looks like. The critical point of this step is that each person within the team sees the success from everyone else's viewpoint, creating a bigger picture in everyone's mind. Each person, each team, brings ideas to the table.

The dentist who owned the practice had each staff member write the successes and improvements they saw in the previous year. Increased patient case acceptance, (i.e. patients accepting their care plans), increased staff utilization in patient care and education, decrease in overhead expenses, and increased collection to production ratio . . . were just a few listed. The exciting part of this step was that everyone started seeing the bigger picture of success, not only their specific piece but also how everyone was involved. They created the belief and feeling of individual, team, and organizational success. For example, one person wrote, "increased collection-to-production ratio" which was also mentioned by someone on the Administrative Team. Staff from other teams realized they had played a part in that success.

Step #2 — Analyzing the Success

As revealed earlier in the Enneagram and dealing in with our primary motivation, the focus is on understanding internal motivation and not just the external behavior. As each person hears the perceptions of the other team members, everyone's viewpoint broadens, creating even more discussion. This step is important as each person on the team starts to realize not only the importance and impact of each individual's part, but the team process of working together, creating interdependence. What will also unfold in this process is the awareness that each success and accomplishment is interdependent. For example, in the dentist's office the increased collection-production ratio was interdependent on increased patient case acceptance as well as increased staff utilization in patient care and education.

Step #3 — Taking the Success to Another Level

The goal of this step is to help the group realize and visualize the next level of accomplishment/success. It has been said, "If you don't know where you're going, how do you know you've ever arrived?" If the team can see what the next level looks, feels, and sounds like, putting a plan in action will be more effective and easier to implement. Most teams are satisfied with the current success, but can we truly afford to be complacent with only one level of success? Due to increased competition in the marketplace, clients expect more today. Effective teams will want to move into the twenty-first century always reaching for the next plateau, yet never forgetting to celebrate their current successes along the way.

Through deliberation, the dental office staff decided what the next level of success looked, felt, and sounded like. Their two key components were: New patients will make appointments based upon referrals from our satisfied and loyal patients and The staff will work from the mindset of accuracy and efficiency: "Let's do it right the first time."

The doctor and staff will offer the latest in dental therapies.

The doctor will invest in the newest dental technologies.

Step #4 — Brainstorming Ideas

This is the time to encourage ideas to fly! The first rule of thumb is "NO idea is to be criticized or analyzed." The moment it is said about an idea, "That won't work," or "We've tried that before," the creativity of the team shuts down. This is a time for people to be a little wacky, creating a variety of ideas. At this time each team member writes ideas. They are sharing what they believe will help the business move to the next level of success. This will stimulate ideas in everyone during this sharing process.

Brainstorming can be implemented in many ways. Mindmapping, storyboarding, or cluster cards are the best ways to get the most mileage out of people and their ideas.

Mindmapping focuses on the next level of success, which is written on the center of a large sheet of paper. As people start calling out ideas, the facilitator takes those main categories and draws a spoke-like line from the center circle with subcategories branching off the main category.

Storyboarding is much like card clusters, where people write their ideas on a card. In storyboarding people work together to create ideas and write them on cards, which the facilitator places on the wall.

With card clusters people work individually, writing their ideas on cards and then placing them onto the wall. With the help of the participants, the facilitator, at this point, starts clustering the cards and ideas that would work together or have the same theme.

Each person on the dental team started visualizing his or her role in the newly articulated goals. One of the team's members said, "Let's give them the Red Carpet Treatment. Patients will feel like they've been not at a Holiday Inn practice, but a Ritz Carlton practice." This immediately created a visual for the future. The mindset of great patient care that brings people back and refers others to this practice was created through some great and wacky ideas.

When you arrive at a Ritz Carlton Hotel, they call you by name, especially if you've been a repeat guest. They have also seen a list that morning of the arrivals for the upcoming day. "The Ritz Carlton dental office" must be able to welcome patients by addressing them by their names as they enter the office. To do this the office will have an early morning huddle prior to the business day to discuss any problems from the day before, financial concerns of any patients, any patients that may need additional time, and to remind everyone to have fun.

When checking into the Ritz Carlton, the staff does everything to make it easy and speedy. The bellman has your luggage and gets your room number from the front desk so that he can immediately take your luggage up to your room, leaving you free to do other things. For the dental office this means checking the patients' charts for any need of updates and making sure the patient cases are completed. When the patients arrive, they receive a warm greeting. They are immediately reminded of the type of insurance they have and questioned for any updates so that the patients' claims can be handled as easily and effectively as possible.

At the Ritz Carlton the concierge informs guests of interesting activities. They also let you know if there is anything special going on within the hotel. They educate you. Education is a very important part of a dental practice. What's important for a practice of this level is not only educating verbally, but educating visually and kinesthetically. This office decided not only to have pamphlets in the patient waiting room, but a TV that would show short clips of videos explaining the cosmetics of dentistry, the steps in a root canal, or the process of getting a crown. What the office wanted as well was to allow the patients to be able to touch and feel such products. They decided to have dentaforms, models of teeth, for patients to look at and play with as assimilations of the actual thing.

During your stay at the Ritz Carlton, every guest room has a survey for you to complete regarding your stay and their service. The Ritz Carlton cares about service and is continuously looking for ways to improve. The dental office decided to send various letters:
- New patient letter sent after initial call and appointment made,
- New patient letter sent after initial visit,
- Patient letter sent after completion of treatment,
- Follow-up calls from the doctor the evening after an emergency.

They also decided to send postcards to let patients know how much they appreciated their business, to reinforce any patient education, and to attract referrals.

Step #5 — Pros and Cons

Now it's time for the team members who are good at trouble shooting to help the team see not only the pluses of an idea but the negatives and challenges that might be encountered. After the ideas are consolidated and combined, each final idea is written on an individual sheet. Team members start discussing the pros and cons of one idea at a time, staying focused so that the process is more effective. As the team members hear each other's particular optimism or concerns, the process of working together toward a new success diminishes potential resistance. Resistance to change or new ideas is usually due to a specific concern that someone has. When people are able to express their concern, they believe they've been heard but may also realize that the concern is not as big as they first thought. This process not only allows a team to come to a conclusion in a group manner, it helps them to visualize a clearer picture.

What also unfolds in this step is that the person who has spoken up with the concern hears the other people coming up with solutions. This helps everyone move away from the problem and find solutions. People start feeling validated.

Step #6 — Appropriate Solutions

Effective teams realize at this point that any choice they make will have some risk. The more the team has discussed the next level of success, the more they have analyzed it openly, effectively and thoroughly, the clearer this step will become. During this step the team views the concerns by discussing ways to deal with the potential problems before they arise. More than one solution may be selected.

The dental staff settled for several of the main ideas that had been synergized. They had the mindset of the Ritz Red Carpet office. They needed to be a facility that was as professional and welcoming as the

Ritz Carlton. They also needed to update their advertising and marketing materials to reflect the image of the Ritz Carlton.

Step #7 — Develop a Plan

Sounds simple, yes? The team at this point will have a clear picture of where they're going based on the previous steps. Standards need to be set to minimize any misunderstanding. Individual responsibilities need to be clearly stated.

The important requirement at this step is to develop a thorough plan that will involve the entire team. The plan needs to address who is going to implement the task, what needs to be accomplished, when it needs to be completed with an awareness of consequences if the task is not done, and how the accomplishment needs to be done. If additional training or resources are needed to accomplish the task, they should be provided.

Looking at the idea of giving patients the "Red Carpet Treatment," the Administrative Team planned to view the upcoming schedule to make sure they didn't have patients scheduled after a certain time. They also set a time to have the following day's schedule ready. The Restorative Team suggested caring for the instruments throughout the day. The plan also set in motion ways to evaluate if there was an adequate instrument supply. All members of the staff found themselves involved in creating "The Red Carpet."

Step #8 — Do It!

Once a team has gone through this process step-by-step, there is a solid buy-in. When people are part of the decision-making process, they are emotionally and intellectually hooked into the result. What's really important at this time is to set the plan on paper. The dental staff needed to see that "The Red Carpet" was not just a mere wish.

When people don't see the plan come to fruition, morale can be disrupted as people start thinking that their ideas haven't been taken seriously. They begin to think that the process was a waste of time. Plans are created from thought, insights, and ideas; without some form of action or movement, they are wasted. If the plan is not implemented, the next time people are taken through the Proactive Decision-Making Process, they won't take it seriously and will be resistant.

Step #9 — Evaluation and Monitoring

Regular evaluation facilitates the Proactive Decision-Making Process, especially if any problems arise. The problems can be dealt with openly and effectively. Often when a team moves forward with a plan, problems crop up during implementation. What's important at this point is to stay flexible by maintaining an open and proactive mindset. If a problem arises, this step-by-step process can be utilized once again with the mindset concentrated on solving the specific problem.

Initiating a process like this one takes time in the short run, but in the long run keeps the organization focused on the end results and future targets. A proactive philosophy will inevitably move through an infra-structure creating success for everyone who is involved. With this Proactive Decision-Making Process, people will see the organization as one that appreciates their ideas. They will feel "in" on the decision-making process and know their company is sympathetic to their per-spectives and viewpoints, empowering success for all.

A special thanks to Neil Blindauer, Branch Manager of Electrohome, who helped me develop another mindset regarding the Proactive Decision-Making Process. This reinforced my own beliefs that it takes each one of us working together to create success at any level.

Also, a special thanks to John F. Dahm, D.D.S. for believing in the Proactive Decision-Making Process and sharing his dental practice and successes with us.

ABOUT
DEBORAH L. DAHM

*F*or over 20 years Deborah Dahm has shared her wit and expertise as an internationally known speaker, trainer and author. She works with corporations, associations and government agencies. Deborah has helped thousands to maximize their effectiveness in relationships, leadership, communication and management of time. Her presentations and encounters include valuable information and light-hearted enthusiasm that leave a positive lasting impact.

From her nurturing nature as a nurse and mother, Deborah Dahm holds key values in her life that she imparts through her presentations and writings:

— Involvement with people and making a difference in their lives,

— Love of challenges and solving life's problems,

— Belief in our power to make choices, and

— Growth from reading and new knowledge.

Deborah is a past president of the Kansas City Chapter of the National Speakers Association.

Contact Information:
Deborah Dahm
Accredited Seminars and Presentations
3315B Covington Court
Hutchinson, KA 67502
phone: (316) 663-3371
fax: (316) 663-3372
e-mail: DLDahm@midusa.net
web: www.DebListens.com

ACCOMPLISH MORE
WHEN YOU LOVE YOURSELF
AND YOUR WORK

by Valerie Y. Jones, M.B.A.

We are in the midst of a revolution in technology, society, economics, and global interdependence. Our fast-changing workplaces and homes require us to be nimble on our feet, to adapt our skills, and to modify our attitudes in order to survive and thrive so that we achieve the kind of lives we truly enjoy. The old models may no longer suffice, so what's needed is a different perspective to help us chart effective courses in order to accomplish our objectives.

Artists understand perspective. The best ones know that reality can be viewed from many different directions or points of view. For example, they may view a subject from the top, left side, right side, or bottom as Picasso did in *Les Demoiselles d'Avignon*. For many of us though, we tend to readily accept the reality, or perspective, of those who raised us, and then we dedicate the rest of our lives to finding comfort by living that reality.

What perspectives might you be trying to live up to? I remember being told that I should "fit in." I think you know what I mean: don't laugh too loudly in public, don't wear colors that are too "crazy," don't do things that might make you look foolish. The message is, "Fit in." The Japanese have an old proverb that sums up this point:

"The nail that sticks up gets hammered down."

I remember a children's story that early on framed one of my perspectives. Maybe you know it, too. A stork delivered babies to expectant mother sheep waiting anxiously in the meadow. It so happened that Mr. Stork was short one baby lamb. To remedy his immediate challenge, he reached into his baby bag and produced a baby lion. The cub, not knowing any better, cuddled up with the mother and bonded. The mother sheep adored him and because she loved him, raised her new baby as she knew best. Growing up in the meadow, he ate like a sheep and tried his best to sound like a sheep. If he did anything that was unsheeplike, he was reminded he was a sheep. Seeing his mother and siblings as sheep, he fought his inner consciousness. In order to fit in and be accepted, he wasn't true to himself. He fought to coerce his brain into proving he was a sheep. How frustrating! How many of us have accepted our role as sheep? How many of us have failed to scrutinize our own talents and gifts because we've been told a version of "You're only a sheep."

I know that part of my purpose in life is to help others by instructing them in ways to maximize their abilities so they love the life they are living. (John F. Kennedy said, "Happiness is the full use of one's abilities along the lines of excellence.") I've had the pleasure of working closely with hundreds of people who are carefully navigating their paths through their personal and professional lives. I've observed first-hand that being successful involves more than strategic positioning, tactical redeployment, and acquiring large sums of money. Various polls report that 30% to 50% of North Americans would change their line of work if they had a chance. Thankfully, more people today are taking that chance! As Marsh Sinetar says in the title of her book, *Do What You Love, the Money Will Follow*.

I have learned there are four key elements involved in loving yourself and your work, and they lead to higher accomplishment.

Know Thyself

Those who know others are intelligent;
Those who know themselves have insight.
Those who master others have force;
Those who master themselves have strength.

— Lao Tzu, *The Tao of Power*

People are becoming more sensitive to their emotional needs. Consequently, the boundaries separating different areas of life are changing. When we were children, we divided the world into neat, well-defined segments: there was school time, play time, television time, meal time, etc. Now as adults, some of us tend to divide ourselves up into "life boxes": work life, family life, spiritual life, civic life, entertainment life, etc. And far too often we end up with disconnected lives which result in disconnected families, disconnected communities, and a disconnected world. But many of us are growing beyond that. Now we can see the boundaries of our boxes easily overlap and an age of a more interrelated view of our lives is dawning — a world where we recognize that we are dependent on all aspects of our lives to be working optimally for happiness, fulfillment, true success, and accomplishment.

Advertising agencies have noticed this emerging consciousness in the general population, as reflected in Volvo's advertising slogan, "Save the Body. Ignite the Soul." Commercials by companies such as Johnson & Johnson and Toyota include inspirations for the soul. From recruiters to advertisers, many are discovering that what resonates with people is recognition that a whole person resides in the body. I refer to our maturing mind set as The Age of Connectedness. In other words, people are waking up from their trance and paying attention to their inner guidance after noticing the hugely dysfunctional environment many live in. We are becoming conscious of our interconnectedness.

Gold ore is heated under pressure at extremely high temperatures to melt away the other minerals and release the gold. You and I are like gold, and adversity is like the heat and pressure. You can stay strong under intense heat and pressure, and when the work is done, know that your gold has been harvested from the ore. Life's challenges require us to go deep — discarding that which is no longer sufficient and revealing that which is essential, that which is the precious treasure of the spirit. The next time you experience a difficult part of your life journey, I suggest, instead of thinking "Why me?" you may want to consider "What have I to learn from this experience about me?" "What treasures are still being developed?" "What seed is yet to bloom?" Mother Teresa understood this gift of discovery when she coyly said, "I know God won't give me anything I can't handle. I just wish He didn't trust me so much."

Weave Your Life as a Rich Fabric

Everyone of us harbors vague memories from long ago that stay etched in our minds. Here's one of mine that's been lingering for 25 years. Robert was a college friend that I knew briefly and with whom I enjoyed exchanging great philosophical conversations. One day he said, "I like your fabric."

"What?" I replied, not understanding.

"I like your fabric," he repeated again.

"What are you talking about?" I asked as I looked down at what I was wearing, more puzzled than ever at this curious statement.

"I like your texture," he said. "You know. Different fabrics have different feels because they're made with different size threads. They're woven differently. Well, I like the way you put things together, the way you think, the way you carry yourself. I like your fabric!"

Then I realized he wasn't talking about my clothes but about my personality. I guess that exchange has resided in my long-term memory for all these years because it was truly one of the best compliments I have ever received. It was a lovely gift he gave to me.

I want you to look at the fabric of your being and the texture of your life. The next time you look at a tapestry or a piece of upholstered furniture, look at the fabric. The ones that stand out often have a weave of many multi-colored, exquisite threads. Notice how the various threads and colors add to the richness. Similarly, think about your life. Do you consciously weave together your work, home, spiritual, and civic lives in a rich texture? Or do you struggle to keep the threads separate? Is your life somehow separate from your work, separate from your fulfillment, separate from family, separate from the society we live in? If separate, then it should not surprise you if you continue to fill up your life with activity in hopes that something will begin to form the glue to hold it all together. Some people hope that activity and adrenaline addiction will keep them from noticing the emptiness that comes from a life that lacks the connectedness of self, livelihood, family, community, and spirit. I say blend them fully and enjoy the diversity! When you do so, you are living all out, throttle fully open, engines full steam ahead! The age of connectedness is here.

Do What You Are Afraid To Do

Do you easily recall when you set out to do something you were afraid to do? Was it going off to college? Asking someone for a date? Interviewing for a job? Changing careers? Recall the fear, the exhilaration, the uncertainty, and then the triumph of overcoming the fear.

I clearly recall a scary experience that taught me a valuable lesson. With a friend, I took a trip to Acapulco, and one gorgeous tropical morning we boarded a catamaran for an excursion with a small group. Off the shore of a small island we dropped anchor into deep water and climbed into a small dinghy for transport to the beach where we had lunch. After lunch, everyone in the group decided to swim back to the catamaran. The thought panicked me as I was not a strong swimmer and had always refused to swim anywhere that I could not reach safely within a few strokes. I decided I would swim with the group, thinking that if I swam on my back I could breathe easily. I received the assurance that my new friends would keep a watchful eye on me.

Halfway from shore to the boat, my ungraceful swimming style exhausted me. I started flailing my arms harder to speed up getting to the boat. The wild motions caused me to splash what felt like gallons of water in my face. To compensate, I threw my tired arms harder into the water. As the water drenched my face and ran into my nose, I gasped for clear breathing. Fear was on the verge of paralyzing me as I imagined drowning so far from home. I talked quietly to myself, "Valerie, you can do this. Be strong. You can do this. Calm down. You can do this. Don't panic. You can do this. God is with you. You can do this." Within a few minutes — which seemed like forever — I did it! Pulled into the safe catamaran, I took in a deep breath of victory, cried, laughed, and my chest swelled with pride. I was so happy I had accomplished this conquest of my fears! You, too, can make a huge step toward achieving a life you love by facing your fears in order to conquer them.

Dudley Lynch and Paul Kordis, co-authors of *Strategy of the Dolphin: Scoring A Win in A Chaotic World* have a great list of examples for doing things that you are afraid of, such as advertise what you usually hide, do alone what you usually do with others, and complete an unpleasant but beneficial task. My personal favorite is trusting my instincts more. When I stay connected with myself and my surroundings, I am able to effectively use my instincts to guide me.

Set Time For Solitude

There is no better way to get connected to all the gifts, the talents, the tools, senses, and traits that you have, than to set aside time for solitude and silence. In most of the seminars that I conduct, participants have told me they found this concept has been hugely helpful in allowing them to create, reflect, and access guidance and direction for their future. People who believe that the highway to greater accomplishment is swiftly traveled with greater activity perceive using solitude to accomplish significant goals as counter-intuitive and useless, particularly in Western cultures. Yet in Eastern cultures, where high technology is as much a part of their modern lives as ours, there is widespread acknowledgment of the benefits of solitude and silence. Whether you take 20 minutes in the morning, a walk at lunch, or sit on the hood of your car and watch the evening sunset, you will find that being quiet and still will reap you significant peace and energy. If you find yourself lamenting that you don't have the time to indulge in solitude, then start by turning off the car radio and enjoy your commute time for this purpose. Pay attention to the little thoughts and whispers of inspiration that come to you. Don't let them get away. Use a recorder or note pad to capture your insights. Shhh! The divine in you speaks quietly, and you can only "hear" in the silence.

There has been no better time than now for you to consciously weave your roles into one role — being you. You'll gain perspective, energy, and peace as you discover your substance, meaning, and purpose. You'll accomplish more when you love yourself and your work. This is the time for which your life has been in preparation. Listen to the calling of your spirit. Be courageous. Be true. Stay connected. Life will bless you with exquisite rewards.

ABOUT
VALERIE Y. JONES, M.B.A.

Valerie Jones, M.B.A., facilitator, speaker and trainer, is President of Resource Consulting. She works with organizations to increase sales and productivity by creating an inspired, connected work environment. The company provides employee selection, development and retention services including team building, leadership and communication seminars. Valerie holds a Master's degree in Business Administration from Columbia University and a B.A. in Economics from Spelman College. The mother of two sons, Valerie credits her work with children of all ages with teaching her valuable lessons on leadership.

Contact Information:
Valerie Jones
Quantum Resource Consulting
165 Shady Brooke Walk
Fairburn, GA 30213
phone: (770) 461-9042
fax: (770) 461-9043
e-mail: VYJones@aol.com

Make That "Jump Now": Conquer Procrastination to Accomplish What You *Really* Want

by Carol Pierce, M.Ed.

Are there changes you would like to implement in your department or your organization? Are you considering switching careers to pursue your true passion? Are you contemplating beginning your own business? What do you want to accomplish? Why don't you have it yet? Why are you procrastinating?

You do have legitimate reasons for procrastination. Discover what they are; determine why you procrastinate; and, more importantly, uncover what you can do to overcome procrastination. Learn how to make that "jump now." By following eight simple steps, you can accomplish what you REALLY want personally and professionally. Is it easy? Not at first. Will it happen overnight? No. Does it work? Yes, if you want it badly enough. The "Jump Now" Steps to Achieve What You REALLY Want are:

Step 1 — Determine what you *really* want.

Step 2 — Expect obstacles.

Step 3 — Determine how badly you want to achieve your goal.

Step 4 — Maintain a positive attitude.

Step 5 — Associate with positive people.

Step 6 — Enter trusting relationships.

Step 7 — Do what is right for you.

Step 8 — Trust in your Higher Power.

Are you ready to conquer your procrastination problems? Are you ready to make that "jump now" to accomplish what you really want? Here's how!

Step 1 — Determine What You REALLY Want

Procrastination is preventing you from accomplishing what you want. Why are you procrastinating? Maybe you don't know what you *really* want. If you are not sure what you really want, how can you get it? The first critical step to climb in making that "jump now" is not to determine what you want; instead, it is to *determine what you really want.*

My friend Becky always dreamed of owning a wellness spa. Just a few months ago, the doors of opportunity opened for her. A building being leased by a local orthopedic surgeon became vacant. After inspecting the facility, Becky knew this would be the ideal spot for her wellness spa. Located in pleasant surroundings, the building needed no structural changes, was convenient to major cities in the region, and was only 35 minutes away from an international airport. It was exactly what Becky had been wanting. At the same time, Becky's mother was moving to another state and needed someone to manage both her arts and crafts shop and her frame shop.

So Becky agreed to manage her mother's two businesses. She also decided to move her own massage therapy business to the newly vacated building. Becky excitedly began planning the conversion of that building into a wellness spa.

Becky thought she knew what she wanted. Three months later, local experts were presenting workshops and seminars at Becky's spa, but Becky was still providing massage therapy at the old location. Why hadn't she moved? Why was she procrastinating? The procrastination was proving costly to Becky, economically and physically.

Becky hadn't yet determined what she really wanted. After three months of frantically trying to operate in three different locations several miles apart, she could no longer handle the stress. Then Becky realized the new spot was large enough to accommodate all the services of the wellness spa and the addition of the frame shop. Because the arts and crafts business was not as profitable, Becky resolved to stock only a limited number of supplies, ordering the rest as her customers needed them. Once she realized what she really wanted, Becky finally progressed to the next step and jumped forward with her plans to create an internationally renowned wellness spa.

You know what you want, but maybe you have not accomplished that goal yet because you have been procrastinating. Is it because you are not sure what you really want? Think carefully about that point. Once you reach your conclusion, you can then climb to the next step so you can "jump now" to accomplish your goal.

Step 2 — Expect Obstacles

Once you have determined what you *really* want, obstacles are guaranteed to appear. When they appear, you again begin to procrastinate. Why now? After all, you do know what you *really* want. But are you prepared to encounter the obstacles that surface? *Expect obstacles* to appear.

Becky was unprepared for the obstacles in her climb. She knew the former clinic needed no major structural changes to be transformed into a spa. The building was handicapped-accessible. Running water and sufficient electrical outlets were available in all the necessary areas. The seminar room even had a fireplace to create the serenity Becky envisioned for her clients. A fresh coat of paint, some interior decorating, and a sign advertising the location seemed to be all that was needed to accomplish her goal.

Prior to the official opening of the spa, I was scheduled to present a workshop on self-publishing as a sneak preview of the variety of programs to be offered there. The night prior to the presentation, my phone rang. Becky's troubled voice proclaimed, "Carol, we have a serious problem. I came in tonight to check the classroom, and the paint is coming off in layers. I don't know what to do about your workshop tomorrow."

Becky and I agreed the best solution would be to conduct the presentation in another room. Problem solved. For me, yes. For the workshop, yes. For Becky, no! Paint began peeling not only in the seminar room, but in all the other rooms. Latex paint had been used over an oil-based paint. Worse yet, a fire had caused considerable damage to the building years earlier. Proper preparation had not been done to much of the damaged areas, so no paint would adhere to the surfaces. Becky had not anticipated these obstacles. Procrastination was about to raise its ugly head.

Becky hired an experienced painter to strip the peeling walls, prepare the damaged surfaces, and repaint the entire interior. She purchased attractive patio furniture, a luxurious fountain, and fragrant candles to create tranquility within the spa. Her sister, who is an artist, painted a serene garden scene in the reception area. But, Becky had no sign along the highway to announce her new location.

Becky continued procrastinating about mounting a sign. The local chamber of commerce held a ribbon cutting to announce the opening of Serenity Wellness Spa. Several people couldn't find the place because there was no sign along the highway. Workshops were being conducted at the place, but some participants had difficulty locating the facility. Becky still had no sign at the highway.

What was the problem? Why was Becky procrastinating about the sign? She simply had difficulty facing all the obstacles surfacing. Becky wanted her clients to have a favorable impression of Serenity Wellness Spa from the moment they entered until the time they left. She felt embarrassed to have them see the place in what she perceived as disarray.

However, individuals coming to the workshops and visiting Serenity Wellness Spa were awed by the facility and its potential. On the exterior, the place looked terrific. On the interior, the painting problems only created a minor distraction to the loveliness Becky had already created. The painting problems posed a dilemma for Becky, but not for her clients.

Becky soon realized that her procrastination in ordering the sign was causing the loss of potential business because people had problems finding her new location. As I walked into Serenity Wellness Spa one day to present a workshop on domestic violence, Becky greeted me with, "Carol, look at the sign I ordered today. It should be up in two weeks!" Becky finally gained victory over her own procrastination.

What unexpected obstacle is preventing you from accomplishing what you really want? Is the obstacle really that difficult to surmount or as bad as it seems? Is your procrastination worth the price you are paying? Reexamine your actions and the results being produced. You may be surprised at what you discover.

Step 3 — Determine How Badly You Want to Achieve Your Goal

When confronting the obstacles in your path, you must *determine how badly you want to achieve your goal.* If you don't want it badly enough, you will procrastinate; you will not attempt to overcome the obstacles. You may even give up at this point. But, if you know what you *really* want and want it badly enough, you will expect obstacles. You will be prepared to surmount any which appear, no matter how difficult. Sometimes, those obstacles will create sufficient pain to force you into taking action.

Becky wanted her wellness spa to become reality. But was the stress really worthwhile? Becky felt frazzled trying to manage the arts and crafts business and the frame shop in one town and her own massage therapy business in another part of the same town while attempting to get Serenity Wellness Spa off the ground in the neighboring community.

For three months Becky procrastinated over solving her dilemma. But the procrastination proved beneficial. When Becky could no longer endure the pain of scattering herself into too many places, she realized she needed to make decisions. The arts and crafts business was not profitable. It was taking time away from what she really wanted to accomplish — establishing Serenity Wellness Spa. However, the frame shop business was lucrative. So Becky decided to relocate the frame shop in a separate part of the building housing the spa. The frame shop would then stock only a few art supplies. Becky would order the remainder on client demand.

Leasing the building for the spa while also leasing space for her massage therapy business in another location proved economically unsound. Why keep that business in the old location? Why not move to the new one? Relocating made good financial sense and would allow Becky more time to pursue her true passion.

But another obstacle was also blocking Becky: the interior repainting was not yet complete. However, the stress of operating in three different locations and the unwise economics of the situation forced Becky to quit procrastinating. She resolved to relocate her massage therapy business as soon as that part of the building was repainted. She also insured that the painter would complete that section first!

Why are you procrastinating? Isn't the pain severe enough? Maybe you don't really want to make that jump. Are the obstacles worth the struggle? How badly do you want to accomplish your goal?

Step 4 — Maintain a Positive Attitude

Once you overcome one obstacle, another surfaces, and then another. As you become discouraged, you again procrastinate. Take control. How? If you really want to accomplish your goal, climb the next step. *Maintain a positive attitude.* Rid yourself of negative thinking.

Discovering that I self-published my book *Jump Now, Look Later: New Ways to Beat Your Fears,* many people often ask, "Carol, how do you self-publish? Is it difficult? What does it involve?"

As they begin talking about the book they have been procrastinating about writing, I always respond, "What are you waiting for?"

Their reply: "Well, I'm not a good writer;" or "I'm afraid I can't do it. I don't even know where to begin."

Once we address those fears, they become excited, and their book takes seed.

The more this scenario is repeated, the more I recognize my gift for encouraging people to make that "jump now" so their books can become reality. For over a year, my National Speakers Association mentor, Mary Kay Kurzweg, encouraged me to write a book on self-publishing. She even suggested a title for it. But I procrastinated; I did not follow my own advice, much less Mary Kay's.

Why? Like the people who come to me for guidance, I lacked self-confidence. I didn't believe I was knowledgeable enough to write a book on self-publishing. Yet, Mary Kay felt I should write such a book; people I admired as experts in their respective fields kept turning to me for self-publishing advice, and I had even conducted a very successful Meet the Pro's session on self-publishing for my New Orleans NSA Chapter Speaker School.

Finally becoming attentive to the positive feedback, I realized here was another avenue to pursue what I really wanted — to encourage people to make that "jump now" to achieve what they really want. My fears that I could not write a book on self-publishing were replaced with the positive outlook that I could help even more people reach their dreams if I fulfilled their request to write such a book. After a year of procrastination and a change of attitude, I began writing *Wanna Self-Publish? Here's How.*

Are the messages you are giving yourself negative or positive? If you keep telling yourself "I can't . . . .," then you won't. Reprogram your brain's computer. Replace "I can't" with "I can; I know I can." When you know you can do something, you have no doubts about your success. Continue reminding yourself that you can accomplish what you really want until you gain the confidence to make that jump.

Focus on all the positive results. By locating all her businesses in one spot, Becky can better concentrate her efforts to make her wellness spa reality. Through the multitude of services offered there, she can help people achieve the serenity they desire in all segments of their life. By writing *Wanna Self-Publish*, I can guide people in making that jump to create the book of their dreams. Their book, in turn, can help other people achieve the lives they truly deserve.

What positive results can spring from your accomplishment? Why wait any longer to achieve what you really want? Aren't you worth it? Don't others deserve the positive outcomes that can be produced?

Step 5 — Associate with Positive People

When obstacles become too unbearable, you have trouble remaining positive. You start procrastinating again. Stop! Call on your support system for emergency assistance. Begin to immediately *associate with positive people* — people who want you to excel, people who won't allow you to procrastinate, people who won't allow you to quit. They'll provide the assistance and the encouragement you need at this point. They are critical to your success.

When confronted with seemingly insurmountable obstacles, Becky feared she had made a wrong decision. Procrastination again raised its ugly head. Becky delayed ordering her sign; she postponed advertising vigorously, and she hesitated attending networking events. Becky was losing confidence in herself and in her dream.

Janet, a fellow chamber of commerce member, observed Becky's procrastination. She encouraged Becky to attend chamber networking opportunities. But Becky needed prodding. Janet lured her to one event with the excuse that Becky needed to be there to have her picture taken for a feature article appearing in the next chamber publication. Becky acknowledged she would not have attended the event otherwise. Janet understands how critical networking is to growing a new business. She wants to see Becky succeed. She provides Becky critical positive support.

Like Janet, I also want to see Becky succeed. One day Becky confessed her fear that leasing the building was a mistake because of all the obstacles that kept occurring. "Becky," I replied, "are you going to let those obstacles stop you? Are you going through all this for nothing? Look at your location. It's ideal. Look at the building. It was built for you. You don't even have to make structural changes. Everywhere I go, people ask me about your spa. What about your dream of people flying from all over the world to come to Louisiana and Serenity Wellness Spa? How badly do you want this?"

"OK, I'm not going to allow those obstacles to beat me," Becky responded after being reminded of her dream and all the positive aspects of her business venture. Listening to my comments, she once again focused on the positive instead of the negative.

What is happening to you? Look at the people who surround you at work and at home. Are they negative? Do they drag you down? Do you feel drained when walking away from them? Or, do they have an optimistic attitude? Do your associates try to lift you up when they see you going down? Are you energized around them? The moment you find yourself becoming negative, start surrounding yourself with those positive people who will reenergize you into wanting to make that "jump now" to accomplish your goal.

Step 6 — Enter Trusting Relationships

The project you are undertaking is more complex than anticipated. You become very frustrated. Procrastination sets in again. Realizing you need assistance, recruit only those individuals and organizations with whom you can enter *trusting relationships.* If you trust each other, you collaborate so that each individual involved can succeed. Everyone wants everyone else to be a winner.

My friend Monica Pierre and I oftentimes joke that we are the queens of procrastination. However, we embarked on one project we wanted so badly that we would not allow ourselves or the rest of our team to procrastinate. We created and co-produced our audio tape *Interview with a Survivor: Reclaim Your Life After Abuse* in less than six weeks, a feat that truly amazed us. What was the key to our success? We gathered together a team that we trusted. Everyone wanted everyone else to excel.

As an Emmy Award-winning journalist and media expert, Monica has the gift of making an interview seem like a conversation. While having lunch one day, Monica and I were discussing that gift in relation to her radio and television interviews with me. My being a survivor of domestic violence and the approach of Domestic Violence Awareness Month created the spark that ignited a strong urgency between us to co-produce an audio tape educating people on strategies to make that "jump now" to turn their life around after abuse.

Wanting this audio tape released October 1 to kick-off Domestic Violence Awareness Month, Monica and I knew we needed quick action. Dividing the duties equally, we each took those with which we were more comfortable. Before leaving, we had already determined the necessary steps, the key team members, and the critical timeline to accomplish our goal, less than six weeks away. Procrastination could not enter the picture!

On October 1, Monica and I successfully released *Interview with a Survivor.* How did we accomplish this daunting task? I trusted Monica in making the right decisions concerning her end of the project, and she trusted me. We communicated through e-mail and contacted each other as soon as a problem arose. We employed trustworthy people on our team. These were successful people whom we trusted and who wanted us to succeed, optimistic people who provided support when a problem occurred.

Are all members of your team trustworthy? Are you in constant conflict with each other, or does each member continually cooperate with you and the rest of the team so that everyone is a success? Remember, trust is a key element in eliminating procrastination to accomplish your goal.

Step 7 — Do What is Right for You

A new CEO is hired. The new company philosophy is counter to yours. Your work environment becomes increasingly stressful. Deep down inside, you really want to leave that department or that organization, but you are scared. You begin losing confidence in yourself and in your decision-making. Your health is being affected. You begin procrastinating about the decision you know you need to make. It is time to take the next step. Listen to that gut feeling. *Do what is right for you.*

A few years ago, I faced a similar problem. As a tenured English teacher in the local high school, I was working under a new administration. Their educational philosophy was counter to mine on several key issues. For a full year, I kept expecting them to change their philosophy. I procrastinated taking the action that was truly needed.

As the next school year began, my health became adversely

affected by all the stress in my life, personally and professionally. The pain became too intense. I had to reduce my stress. I finally admitted to myself that I could not change the administration's philosophy. I had to be the one to change. I had to change my job.

So, I took some very shocking action. Even though I am a firm believer in commitment, I broke my contract with the local school board, left my position at the high school during that first week of the new school year, and accepted an adjunct position at the local university. The adjunct position was a temporary one with no guarantee of contract renewal the next semester. The pay was minimal, less than one third of my salary at the high school. My family and my friends were convinced I had jumped into the deep end of an empty pool. But that jump became a swan dive.

Knowing what appeared to be the negative terms of my adjunct contract, I felt completely at peace accepting the job. Yes, the position offered no job security and only a meager income for a single person like me. However, it provided the stress-free environment essential at that point in my life. It also allowed me to provide individual assistance to each of my students. As a bonus, I was surrounded by positive, supportive people, people who helped me survive some of the darkest days of my life. In addition, I now had some free time to begin building my professional speaking and consulting career on a part-time basis. A few years later, my oldest daughter admitted to her mother-in-law, "Ms. Faye, taking that job at Nicholls was one of the best decisions Momma ever made."

Think back to the decisions you have made personally and professionally. When you listened to that little voice, did you feel comfortable with your decision? Was it a wise one? Each time you ignored that little voice, did you feel uneasy with your decision? Was it a poor choice? Quit procrastinating. Develop confidence in yourself. Your inner voice will not lead you astray.

Step 8 — Trust in your Higher Power

Well, you have climbed all the steps so far, and you know your project can be successful. But unexpected problems appear at the last minute, issues completely out of your control. Your entire plan is thrown completely off course. That is no accident. Don't allow procrastination to step into the picture. Something better awaits. *Trust in your Higher Power.*

While writing *Wanna Self-Publish? Here's How,* I realized I could be an even more valuable resource by conducting self-publishing workshops. That was my original plan; however, a better one was waiting.

Only one person registered for that first workshop, so I spent those four hours working one-on-one with Jo Huey, who had been procrastinating about completing her book on Alzheimer's. Jo wanted to release her book at the beginning of National Alzheimer's Awareness month, just three months later, but she had not even brought her manuscript to her editor yet. At the end of our session, an excited Jo left, confident that she could now tackle her procrastination. She knew she could release her book within the three month deadline.

A short time later, I offered a second workshop. Again, only one person registered. Having begun his parenting book in 1986, Greg Young had procrastinated completing it. I spent four intensive hours helping Greg get unstuck with his manuscript so he could make his "jump now." At the end of those four hours, Greg had no doubt about his book being released less than four months later.

Those two workshops taught me a lesson my Higher Power knew I had forgotten — I enjoy teaching people one-on-one and know the effectiveness of individualized attention. I could successfully take Jo and Greg from exactly where they were with their individual books and guide them to where they wished to go because each received the individual attention a one-on-one session allows that would not be possible in a workshop situation.

My experiences with Jo and Greg taught me what I really needed to do — share my self-publishing expertise with people in a one-on-one format, something I had not previously considered My original strategy needed revision. The workshops were not a failure; they were a great learning experience for Jo, for Greg, and for me!

When your plans don't produce the exact results you projected, view it as no accident. Avoid procrastinating. Instead, closely examine what is happening. What new lesson must you learn? What really needs to be accomplished?

Does procrastination have to prevent you from achieving what you really want? No. If you want it badly enough, follow these eight simple steps. You, too, can then make that "jump now" to can accomplish anything you *really* want.

ABOUT
CAROL PIERCE, M.ED.

*C**arol Pierce is an internationally known human relations expert, speaker and author. She is the owner of Success NOW! (a consulting company). She firmly believes that anyone can overcome procrastination and "jump now" to accomplish anything he or she really wants to accomplish. Her eight step "Jump Now" program has worked for many organizations to breakthrough inertia to reach higher levels of achievement. Carol is the author of three books: "Jump Now, Look Later: New Ways to Beat Your Fears;" "The Jump Now Program to Achieving What You Really Want;" and "Wanna Self-Publish? Here's How." She is co-author of "Interview with a Survivor: Reclaim Your Life After Abuse." And her chapter, "Thank You Nicole," from the book "Sisters Together" was featured in* Outlook on Health *magazine.*

Contact Information:
Carol Pierce
Success NOW!
P.O.Box 250
Raceland, LA 70394
phone: (504) 537-5713 or (877) JumpNow
fax: (504) 537-3187
e-mail: Carol@JumpNow.com
web: www.JumpNow.com

DARE TO DREAM: EMBRACE OBSTACLES

by Sharyn Scheyd

You have to have a dream so you can get up in the morning.
— Billy Wilder

But what happens when that dream is shattered? One thing that I have learned in life is that sometimes, we can do all the right things to accomplish our dreams: set goals, develop a vision, keep a journal and work the plans. And then the unexpected happens. An obstacle of insurmountable proportions occurs and throws our life out of control.

Let me tell you a story. Fifteen years ago I had two wonderful sons and was pregnant with my third child. In the delivery room when we learned it was a girl, the staff started jumping for joy. My sons, outside the room, were elated that they had a baby sister.

What a wonderful time to have a girl. It was the coming of age for women; we could be anything we wanted to be. Little Ashley had all the possibilities life had to offer ahead of her. My dreams were becoming reality. Life was good.

When I took Ashley shopping with me, people would stop me on the street and tell me how bright-eyed my daughter was, how intelligent she was going to be. I would agree and say, "Yes, she can even be a brain surgeon."

This turned out to be an ironic choice of careers for Ashley. At four months old, she went into static seizures. After several EEGs and a CAT Scan, we found out that she had Lissencephaly (smooth brain). Most brains look like a walnut, Ashley's looked like a pecan. I was told she would be a "vegetable" and probably not live to be a year old.

My world was shattered; I was totally devastated. But I did not know that this was just the beginning. The next day my middle child almost died from a missed ruptured appendix, gangrene, and peritonitis. The surgeon told me that if we had gotten him into surgery two hours later, he would have died. Within the year, my husband left, and we lost our house and car. Now, as the single mother of three children (one with profound disabilities), working several jobs to make ends meet and starting from below bottom, I was to learn to embrace obstacles.

We have all faced tragedies in our lives. What have been some of the obstacles that you have faced? Did your business go bankrupt, did you get fired, or did you get an unwanted transfer? Do you believe that life will never be good again? Whatever your crisis, you *can* overcome it, learn from it, and go on to live a life with more joy and success than you thought possible. It will be one of the hardest things that you will do, but YOU can accomplish things you never thought possible.

"We who lived in the concentration camps can remember the men
who walked through the huts comforting others, giving away
their last piece of bread. They may have been few in number,
but they offer sufficient proof that everything can be taken from a
man but one thing: The last of his freedoms —to choose one's attitude
in any given set of circumstances, to choose one's own way."
— Viktor E. Frankle
Man's Search for Meaning

When you are in the middle of dealing with a crisis, you may feel that you will not survive. Many out-of-control feelings come up. Strong feelings that can threaten to take over your life. They can sabotage and destroy your dreams if you let them. But, you are in control of your feelings. When I was first told about Ashley, I was angry, sad, and depressed to name a few. When an unexpected obstacle comes along, face your feelings about the situation. Feelings are not right or wrong, but it is what you do with them that makes the difference.

One way to deal with the negative emotions is to go to a quiet spot where you feel comfortable and safe. Ask yourself what you can learn from this experience. How have obstacles in the past made you a better person? Write down what you are feeling. Do not worry about grammar or spelling. Just get in touch with the raw feelings. Writing them down is one safe way to deal with them. Give into the anger, sadness, etc. on paper. Make it as real as possible.

Now that you have identified your feelings, how can you choose to channel them into productive, positive activities? What are some of the ways that you can put these feelings to use to make your situation better? How can you choose your own way?

Actor Christopher Reeve was injured in a horse riding accident in 1995. His acting career seemed to be over. However, he has not only appeared in and directed movies since then, but he has put a lot of his energy into increasing medical research for a cure for spinal cord injures. Many people would have let an accident like this destroy them. Reeve put his energy into reaching his original dream and adding a new dream. He has accomplished the seemingly impossible.

Not long after Ashley was diagnosed, I started a federally funded, state-wide program to educate parents in their rights for their children with disabilities and helped to get State legislation passed that allows children and adults with severe disabilities to remain in their homes and their communities. It took me a long while to get over the negative aspects of the feelings of anger, sadness, and depression, but each day I just put one foot in front of the other and took baby steps until I was able to fully concentrate on my new direction in life.

I can remember asking a friend of mine, Tony, "Do you think that Ashley can be cured?" Tony said, "Yes, but first you must accept Ashley as she is." "I will NEVER, EVER accept this. It is unacceptable," I screamed.

One day while driving home from the legislature, I was thinking about Ashley and realized that she was perfect the way she was. No, she cannot hold her head up or talk, but she radiates happiness. She brings peacefulness to all who come in contact with her. A miracle had happened. She was not cured; I had decided to accept her for who she was.

You always have choices. You may not like any of them, but you always have choices. You can put the energy from your feelings into something healthy or you can stay in the negativity. One thing that will guide you are your values. You may change the direction you are going in, but you always go in the direction of your values. Goals may change, but your values don't.

How will this new situation redirect your dream? Do you need to change your dream completely or just redirect it? One thing is for sure: it is time to get involved in something larger than yourself. Growth comes with each challenge.

"You only lose energy when life becomes dull in your mind.
Your mind gets bored and therefore tired of doing nothing.
Get interested in something! Get absolutely enthralled in something!
Get out of yourself! Be somebody! Do something.
The more you lose yourself in something bigger than yourself,
the more energy you will have."

— Norman Vincent Peale

When you are in a crisis, your energy level is often low. It can be hard to just get out of the bed in the morning. By redirecting your energies into something bigger than yourself, you get out of yourself. You have a new outlook on life. You have a reason to get up.

Emotions that could bring us down can be used to create better lives for ourselves, our family, and our community. We control our thoughts, our thoughts control our emotions, and our emotions control our environment. We are in charge of our lives.

Choose happiness. We know that laughter relaxes the diaphragm, exercises the lungs, and increases oxygen intake. After laughing our muscles are relaxed. Norman Cousins refers to laughter as "internal jogging." Laughter releases endorphins and natural killer cells that destroy viruses and tumors. As I said, do not ignore the bad feelings, but use the energy from them to create momentum in your new direction. Choose happiness and laughter to improve your health and quality of life.

Sometimes, we all need a little help getting out of the bed. Did you ever wake up and just want to throw the covers back over your head and stay there all day? That happened to me last week. Then I thought to myself, "You need to practice what you preach." I put a smile on my face and got out of the bed. I answered the phone with a forced smile in my voice. I dressed in bright clothes for my meeting. Before I knew it, I was having a great day. I forgot that I did not want to get up. I accomplished more than I normally do. Try it! It really works.

Another experiment to try is to think of something that makes you mad, then smile. Can you hold the angry thought and the smile? When I do this exercise in my workshops, no one has been able to do it yet. Our emotions do not choose us; we choose them.

> *"Luckily, most of my problems have never occurred."*
> — Mark Twain

Up to now, we have been talking about real obstacles, life-changing events. How often do you spend time worrying about things that never happen? Will you ever get another sale, fail the test, or ever have another date? What is the worst thing that will occur if these events do happen? You are usually wasting your time worrying about these things. Take action, keep going, and you will find out that usually the event does not happen. When I got divorced, my friends told me that my children and I would be homeless, that I could not afford to provide for my three children. Then when I lost the house and car, I spent an enormous amount of time worrying that my friends' predictions would come true. The amount of time that I spent worrying about impending doom could have been better spent on creating sources of income and enjoying my children.

As it turns out, I was able to get another car and find an apartment in the same neighborhood where we had been living. Worrying had just served to drain my energy and make life miserable. We can never get back the time we spend worrying. Use that time to work toward accomplishing your goal.

> *"The highest reward for a person's toil is not what they get for it,*
> *but what they become by it."*
> — John Ruskin

So, now you are on your way toward accomplishing a new and improved dream. It is not the same one you started with, but I have found that it usually brings you more joy than the original and that you become a better person for having gone through what you have experienced.

I was a medical technologist before Ashley's birth. Since then, I have founded and directed several non-profit agencies (Project PROMPT, Louisiana Guardianship Services, Inc., Interfaith Volunteer Caregivers Program) and become a professional speaker. Before, I was so shy that I thought I was invisible. Now, I love my present life, and I would probably not have gone in this direction if not for the series of crises that I have encountered. The greatest obstacle of my life has brought me the greatest joy.

As for Ashley, she is now fifteen. She is not able to hold her head up, has no speech, is fed by a tube into her stomach, and uses a wheel-chair. She has been a Brownie and Girl Scout, goes to our neighborhood school, and attends regular classes. The children tell me that she is their best friend because they can tell her anything and she does not repeat it to anyone! Children of all ages tell me, "You know, Ms. Sharyn, we are all different. It is OK to be different." Ashley is not a brain surgeon, but she is a teacher. She is teaching us that diversity is good, that we all have gifts to share, and that we must appreciate ourselves for who we are.

It has not been easy, nor is it the journey I would have chosen. But I am a stronger person and happier than I ever thought possible.

Embrace obstacles. You will accomplish things you never thought you could.

ABOUT
SHARYN SCHEYD

*L*egislative *activist, author, consultant and professional speaker —
that's Sharyn Scheyd. Using concrete examples and powerful stories
from real life, she helps individuals clarify and achieve their goals. Sharyn
has founded and directed several non-profit service agencies. She has been
published in Stephen Covey's magazine,* Personal Excellence, *and is a co-
author of "Sisters Together, Stories that Have Anchored Our Souls". She's
a columnist for the magazine* Outlook on Health. *Sharyn's newest audio
cassette learning program is "Dream from Your Heart: How to Become the
Person YOU Choose to Be".*

Contact Information:
Sharyn Scheyd
Sharyn Scheyd, Inc.
P.O.Box 641642
Kenner, LA 70064
phone: (800) 4-SharYn (474-2796)
e-mail: callSharYn@aol.com
web: www.nolaspeaks.com/SharYn

ZERO TOLERANCE FOR MEDIOCRITY

by Rick Phillips

T he Green Bay Packers won only one game in the 1958 football season. They hired rookie head coach Vince Lombardi, who led the team to a winning season in 1959 and the world championship game in 1960. He took a team from a nucleus of mediocrity to uncommon team character, the epitome of football accomplishment and legendary victories in less than two seasons. Just as important, Lombardi pushed (grew) people on his team to accomplishments they never thought were possible.

On examining his management style, players and fellow coaches have politely described him in terms of a firm taskmaster who could occasionally show compassion. He would not, however, allow anyone around him to accept less than his best, and he assumed that people don't know how good they can be, so Lombardi quite simply never settled for less than what he thought was possible for them.

Above all, Vince Lombardi had zero tolerance for mediocrity. After winning his second consecutive Super Bowl, Lombardi took a desk job and was replaced by Phil Bengston, a knowledgeable and qualified coach, who had a different style of management. The next season Bengston led the same team to a mediocre four wins and eight losses. Green Bay did not return to the Super Bowl for 30 years.

Management style does make a difference!

Ask any first year MBA student, and he or she will tell you about the two extreme theories of management.

Theory X management, when taken to its extreme, is essentially an authoritarian model. These impersonal and highly pragmatic managers assume that employees are naturally lazy and irresponsible. They tend to delegate very little authority, have their fingers involved in most decisions, and "empowerment" is not in their vocabulary.

Writer and speaker Hank Tristler says, "Under Theory X management, it is assumed that if brains were gunpowder, then the average employee couldn't blow his nose."

When talking to Theory X managers, I hear them repeat two comments, "You just can't find good people any more" and "People just don't want to work like they used to." My question for them is, "You hired them, you trained them, you developed the environment in which they work . . . the environment that motivates or demotivates them. Tell me who you think has a problem?"

As a result of this style, we commonly see a spiritual malaise of mediocrity in the eyes of workers, and it shows up in reduced productivity and complacency toward the customer.

Theory Y management features much more employee participation and open communications. Managers practicing this style actually seek worker feedback and spend more of their time listening than talking at meetings. These managers work to achieve consensus on decisions, "empower" employees, and implement front-line ideas for change.

While the Theory Y style of management has gained much favorable consideration, critics explain the style is easily mistaken as weakness. They refer to Theory Y as "management by Mr. Rogers."

When taking this theory to its extreme, Theory Y managers face great frustrations. I hear them talk about being "fair" and complaining that "My people show me no respect" and "Employees just don't listen to me."

Somewhere in the middle of these two styles are the practices of the most successful managers in business today, the practices of legendary managers and leaders like Vince Lombardi. We call that style Theory Zero.

Management by Theory Zero

Zero Tolerance for Mediocrity is understanding that the first time you accept mediocrity is the last time you will see excellence. Theory Zero says that you never let people settle for anything less than their best. Mediocrity is the path of least persistence; it's the easy way out. It is the absence of leadership. Allowing mediocrity assigns people to a lack of accomplishment.

The Theory Zero manager gives employees personal and professional respect and empathy, while expecting them to perform to the best of their abilities. The manager (or the work team itself) sets the expectations and passes them on in such a way that people know the high expectations are not arbitrary or debatable but not punitive either.

Rick Gabardy, a former national training manager for Tosco Corporation, explains that "Employees will usually perform up to the manager's expectations."

The future of new employees can take one of two directions: They can decide to find and follow what is the lowest acceptable level of performance, or they can be shown what is possible and directed toward success.

New employees come into the workplace, look around and quickly define what is an acceptable performance level. They want to fit in, to conform. If employees are allowed to drift to the lower side of the scale, their future is in jeopardy.

Nancy Chutz, a British Petroleum store manager says, "If the manager does not teach the employee to accept responsibilities, to perform his or her work assignments as a professional, then the manager is usually assigning that employee to a life as a minimum wage worker."

The manager can lead people into excellence and self-pride by coaching them to understand that Zero Tolerance is non-punitive and at the same time non-negotiable. Theory Zero is coaching the employee to understand that excellence is the only thing that is acceptable, and if you are going to be on this team, you will excel.

Tom Peters and Robert Waterman in their watershed book, *In Search of Excellence*, wrote: "The excellent companies are marked by very strong cultures, so strong that you either buy into their norms or you get out. There is no halfway house."

The best-kept secret in the American workplace today is that people will work hard and smart.

Retailing superstar Nordstrom's is a great example of Zero Tolerance. People who work there face very high expectations (some don't make it) and are given many responsibilities. There are only two employee rules: #1. Use your own best judgment. #2. If you follow rule #1, no other rules are necessary.

The U.S. Marines are a Zero Tolerance outfit. Expectations are high, discipline is unyielding, and the pressure to perform is legendary. But don't try to take that "Semper Phi" bumper sticker off the car of a marine. Marines are a proud and motivated lot because they have been part of a tough and unyielding, worthwhile organization that expects and gets the best out of people. They have learned the truth about teamwork and individual responsibility and passed the test of Zero Tolerance for Mediocrity.

Rules to Remember

#1 You can never not lead.

The beleaguered manager says, "I tell the employees to honor our customers. I tell them that the customer is #1, but we are still losing market share, and I know it's because of poor service habits." And yet this is the manager who avoids calls from complaining customers.

"A business is the reflection of the leader," says Gary Feldman. "A fish doesn't stink just from the tail, and a business doesn't fail from the bottom."

The Theory Zero manager asks, "What am I doing to show the staff where the priorities really are?" Is the manager a demonstration of the principles he wants to see in his employees? Denial is more than just a river in Egypt. Tom Peters reminds us, "They watch our feet not our lips."

I remember many years ago I was guilty of whining about the lack of sales productivity on my team of sales reps. Brent Minor, our vice president of sales, looked me straight in the eyes and said, "Rick, you'll be surprised how good they will get once their manager gets good!"

As a manager, you can never not lead. You can't nail Jell-O to a wall. You can't find a sunrise by walking west. And you can never not lead.

Robin Oldham was the general manager of the Westin Hotel in New Orleans. He was an awesome leader, the captain of his ship. His very "English" management style indicated his no-nonsense, zero tolerance attitude. He maintained a charisma, demonstrating that presence is more than just being there.

After an early morning breakfast briefing Robin and I exited the hotel's cafe on our way to a leadership meeting with the rest of the managers. As we walked at a quick pace, Robin reached down and picked up an almost invisible cellophane wrapper top discarded from a cigarette package. He slipped it into his jacket pocket without a word. He was sending a message. He understood that you can never not lead.

Days later, I was with another hotel general manager at a major hotel. As we neared the elevator, he excused himself and walked to the bell station. There he physically grabbed one of the bellmen and in a not too subtle voice said, "Do you see that candy bar wrapper?" pointing to the offending litter near a cigarette receptacle. He continued, "Haven't I told you about taking pride in this place? When will you people ever learn that image is everything to our customers?"

We never did any leadership training for his hotel. The general manager felt he could handle that on his own. Yes, he was always teaching them something.

You can never not lead.

#2 Do unto your employees, as you would have them do unto your customers.

Who are the most important people to walk through the doors of your business each day? Customers, right? Wrong!

We learned a long time ago, while doing sales training and consulting, that the lowest paid employee on the staff can run off more business than the highest paid salesperson can bring in. Please recognize that how we treat our people will be directly reflected in their attitude toward our customers. It's human nature. And our employees are our business.

Most major cities can be confusing to the unfamiliar driver and Memphis is no different. Lost and anxious to get to a meeting, I stopped Roy, an Airborne Express driver, and asked for his help. After looking at my map for a minute, Roy paused and said, "Follow me." I followed him through a maze of streets for five minutes to get to my destination. He took that time out of his busy delivery day, and he didn't need to be told I spent $3,000 last year on packages sent through Airborne Express.

Airborne is not some fleet of airplanes or some corporate boardroom. Airborne is Roy.

The phone rang in my room at the Houstonian Hotel at 5:30 a.m. and Cynthia's cheery voice on the other end announced the time and reported that it was a "beautiful morning in Houston." She sensed I was quite drowsy and offered, "Mr. Phillips, if you like, I can let you sleep for a few more minutes and call you again."

"A snooze wake-up call?" I asked. Cynthia repeated the offer, and I told her that it wouldn't be necessary but added that I really appreciated the thought. As I hung up the receiver, I realized that I had just been witness to a new experience. Cynthia and the Houstonian Hotel had just introduced me to a new level of service, not born of rules but of real people who take hospitality one step further than they are required to.

An important part of the success of IBM for the past 50 years is the culture of the organization, much of which is based on the legendary lessons in leadership taught by Tom Watson. One of my favorite stories from the Tom Watson era is about the engineer who made a million-dollar mistake. The offending engineer was asked to report to Watson's office, and as he approached the president's desk, he blurted out, "I guess you will be asking for my resignation." "Resignation?" asked the stunned Watson. "I just paid a million dollars getting you an education."

In that split second, Watson sent a message throughout the entire organization: Making a mistake is not fatal as long as we learn something from it. The mistake had already been made. The million dollars was already gone. What would be gained by firing the engineer? The fact is this engineer would not make that mistake again, but his replacement might! Furthermore, firing the engineer would probably make everyone in the organization much more cautious about taking the chances that are necessary when looking for breakthroughs in technology.

On reflection, Watson's response was just good leadership

judgment and common sense, but then Will Rogers reminds us that "Common sense is not that common."

At Phillips Sales and Staff Development, we teach a five-step process to improve or correct performance.

1. Expectations: Let employees know what you expect. Have a dialogue that explains the requirements for the task. Let them ask questions and insure that they understand what you expect. Later, if expectations are not being met, assume you have not been clear. Let's face it, when people fail, they are not doing it just to annoy the boss.

2. Skills/Knowledge: Insure that employees know how to do the job and that they have the tools necessary to be successful.

3. Obstacles: Remove any impediments that would prevent or delay the successful accomplishment of the task. (Employees define the obstacles.)

4. Feedback: Let people know how they are doing. Feedback, positive and formative, is critical to anyone's growth. Positive feedback lets people know when they are doing well; this stimulates confidence and job satisfaction while increasing productivity. At the same time, people need to know when they have gotten off track and how to correct their problems. We call this formative feedback; we are "forming" correct behaviors and work habits. As Joe Noblett, a training supervisor at Standard Motor Products, likes to say, "Anyone can walk on water, if they know where all the stumps are."

5. Consequences: Positive consequences may be as simple as a pat on the back and a direct comment on the correct behavior. Never a vague comment like, "You've been doing good." Instead, make specific statements like, "You handled that last transaction very well. You asked the customer the right questions and were able to direct her to just the right person. Good job." Negative consequences are also necessary. The first rule of Theory Zero is understanding that the first time you accept mediocrity is the last time you will see excellence. If starting time is 8:00 a.m. and nothing is said to an employee who arrives at 8:05, then the message is, "While 8:00 is the official starting time, the new acceptable starting time is 8:05." The bar is set where the manager allows it to be set.

Handling negative consequences is perhaps one of the touchiest subjects in management. And the word we use is "proportionate." The first time Angela is late, perhaps the manager will ask her into his office and simply remind her, without listening to excuses, that 8:00 is starting time. Others in the office need to see that the boss addressed Angela's tardiness. Incidentally, negative consequence conversations are never conducted in front of other employees.

Once they have clear rules and expectations, get the employees involved in decisions. Let them talk about your expectations and let them know it is OK to take chances. They will understand the rules and know when flexibility is necessary, and they will know when breaking the rules is correct and important. They will also know they can question your expectations, and the employees will make a very positive impact in the organization.

Goethe said: "Treat a man as he appears to be and you will make him worse. But treat a man as he was already what he could potentially be and you will make him what he should be."

#3 Never Settle.

My friend and mentor, the late John Ulmo, used to tell managers that "The greatest enemy of excellence is good." Too often we settle for "good" when excellence is possible. When the only standard of performance is excellence, people can accomplish unreasonable and great things.

In sports we have hundreds of examples of athletes who did not settle for good enough. Gail Deavers won an Olympic gold medal 13 months after being diagnosed with Graves disease and being told she would need to have her feet amputated.

On September 14 of 1993, New York Yankee pitcher Jim Abbot won a "no hitter," a feat that is accomplished only once or twice a year in major league baseball. But what makes it incredible is that Jim Abbott has only one arm.

They had goals that seemed impossible to most. They looked beyond what people assume is reasonable to what they thought was possible and then decided that they could not settle for less. We call that unreasonable logic; they call it accomplished.

George Bernard Shaw tells us that: *"The reasonable man adapts himself to the world; the unreasonable one persists in trying to adapt the world to himself. Therefore all progress depends upon the unreasonable man."*

Nestor Corporation, a sales and distribution company in Tampa Bay, has nearly 100,000 parts and products in their massive warehouse and one overriding philosophy of business: "Order by 1:00, out by 5:00." That's unreasonable!

Ready to challenge this unreasonable approach, I asked company president John Cross how often they manage to ship full orders with that kind of commitment to speed. When he said 98.3 percent of the time, I had to ask how in the world they reached that unreasonable level of service. He said, "We reached 98.3 percent by falling from 98.5 percent and we fell to 98.5 percent after settling for 98.8 percent. That's why you are here."

Dave Carriere of Centennial Foods in Calgary says: "We see our jobs as making the unreasonable possible. We can't settle for anything less. My customers are not reasonable about their expectations. My competition is not reasonable. So I can't be reasonable either. The fact is we can't really know what is unreasonable until we have tried it."

In the New Orleans Riverwalk shopping center a fudge shop

attracts non-stop business. Someone built a culture where the young employees are constantly coming up with ways to make what they do fun for them and their customers. They sing about fudge; they dance behind the counter and play while preparing the fudge. And customers are eating it at astronomical prices. That's unreasonable. The product is way too expensive, and, by the way, where do you find young people today willing to work and put on a floor show for minimum wages? That's unreasonable.

There is another candy shop in the Riverwalk. It features bored and apathetic employees like those we see in many retail organizations. This store's culture is shallow and laden with rules. Instead of inviting excitement and innovations, the employees are told to obey instead of grow. They have never been asked their opinion nor have they been asked to take an active part in the store. They are told, in so many words, to show up and shut up.

One of the greatest dangers this country faces is the under-utilized employee. Employees in the Japanese electronics industry submit 54 suggestions per employee each year. At the same time American employees submit .7 suggestions. In too many cases, front-line people who are intimately familiar with the details of their work are not contributing their ideas to promote productivity. They continue to tell us that "Nobody listens to me, so why even try?"

We can't accept or settle for employee complacency that is rooted in old management practices. When employees are involved and empowered in the organization, they will contribute and buy into the future of the organization. In today's world economy we cannot settle for minimum contributions from any employee. And to accept less is a disservice to the employee who is never given the chance to contribute and grow to his or her potential.

Once you ask employees to look beyond what most people assume is reasonable to what is possible, you have to become an advocate for their ideas. You will have to be an active listener and a participant in the change. Employee motivation and trust are fragile and circumstantial and are the responsibility of the manager.

An old maxim urges us to get the best from our employees:

The Edge

He beckoned them to the edge, they came.
He told them it would be difficult, they agreed.
He pushed them, they flew.

Because they can fly, it is up to the manager to prove it to them, to push employees past what they think is possible. Henry Kissinger said the "task of the leader is to get his people from where they are to where they have not been." To compromise that calling is to compromise the manager's own character.

Finally, we need to recognize that the impact of Zero Tolerance for Mediocrity stretches far beyond the doors of our businesses. It reaches into the very fabric of our country since the only standard of performance that can sustain a free society is excellence.

ABOUT
RICK PHILLIPS

*T*he *author of more than 100 articles on sales and customer service, Rick Phillips shares his wealth of sales and management experience. He has been a salesman in small business and a senior executive in Fortune 500 businesses. Known for his fast paced, enthusiastic and humorous style, Rick has spoken to groups throughout North America. He delivers high content, orginal material that is highly interactive and stimulating. His training engenders results for organizations of all sizes. His clients include Hilton Hotels, Chevron, duPont, IBM, Monsanto, Entergy, Exxon, State Farm Insurance, and many others, including Tulane and Clemson Universities.*

Contact Information:
Rick Phillips
Phillips Sales and Staff Development
P.O.Box 29615
New Orleans, LA 70189
phone: (800) 525-PSSD (7773)
e-mail: PSSD@web-net.com
web: www.RickPhillips.com

WHY GOOD LISTENERS
ACCOMPLISH MORE

by Maureen Murray, M.S.Ed.

D o you remember the kindergarten game "Telephone" in which the children sat in a circle, and the teacher whispered something to the first child, who then passed it along to the next, and so on until everyone had a turn? When the final child relayed the message back to the group, it bore little resemblance to the original. "Tommy has a yellow goose" became "Tommy has smelly shoes" and "Susan is baking a chocolate cake for her Dad" translated into "Susan is breaking the chalk because she's mad." How we laughed at those breakdowns in communication!

Back then we took delight in our lack of rudimentary listening skills. In fact, some of the more daring among us actually tried to scramble the message to get a few laughs. But an experienced teacher is nobody's fool, and, after the hilarity died down, she talked to us quietly for a few minutes about the importance of being good listeners. (She was ahead of her time about learning everything you need to know in kindergarten.) By the end of the year we thought we had made great strides and proudly took home "Good Listener" awards for posting on our refrigerator doors.

The overwhelming majority of us genuinely believe that we are excellent listeners — and many of us are — so we act in good faith and conduct our personal and business relationships accordingly. But could we be listening at an even higher level? Are we using the most effective listening style for each situation? Are we pausing long enough for the speaker to finish the message? And is our level of listening skill supporting what we want to accomplish?

In my years of work at a family mental health center and as a private practice counselor, I spent a great deal of time listening and made some important discoveries about the process. In my career as a keynote speaker and trainer — because I was doing most of the talking — I learned some even more subtle things about "listening" to audience reactions. The most significant thing I realized is that good listeners are made, not born, and that the thoughtful application of some basic principles made an enormous difference.

Good listening is a basic building block of accomplishment. The more effectively I listened to my clients in counseling sessions, the greater progress we made toward goals. The more I "heard" my audiences, the more people came to the podium afterwards and made comments such as "You said what I needed to hear," or "Your remarks really gave me perspective," or "I learned a lot today." People were telling me that I had successfully conveyed information or touched their lives. I felt both humbled and grateful to have attained my goals.

Listening well will help you accomplish your goals, too. Whether you're a supervisor or a salesperson, a coach or a consultant, a trainer or a technician, good listening skills will set you on the path to attaining your dreams.

Why Good Listeners Really Do Accomplish More

Think about the people you know who set goals and accomplish them almost effortlessly, who attract golden opportunities, who keep getting better in both their careers and their personal relationships. They appear to have a minimum of conflict in their lives, and when it does arise, they handle it skillfully and there they go, steaming ahead toward their goals again. Sure, they have their challenges and troubles, but why does it seem that they know the right contacts who can help them? Where are they getting all those strong supporters and allies who come to their aid. Why are they able to resolve their difficulties in such a timely way and then move on? One reason is that they are good listeners!

The relationship between listening and accomplishment is directly proportionate to the skill of the listener. Good listeners accomplish more than average or poor listeners for several reasons.

1. Good listeners build supportive relationships.

The human need to be heard and understood runs deep.. Consider the millions of people who visit counselors, psychologists and psychiatrists. While their perceived need is to find a solution to a problem, their primary and fundamental need is to have someone who will listen to them in a focused, non-judgmental, and empathic manner. Good therapists know that the client must first feel connected and understood before any solutions can be explored. Listening with empathy — that is, listening to understand the person's feelings and not just to gather information — causes a profound transformation to occur. When we are truly heard and understood, we feel affirmed, significant, worthwhile. Moreover, we develop strong loyalty to the people — the exceptional listeners — who provide us with this extraordinary experience.

That's one reason why the accomplishers gather that remarkable collection of loyal supporters, allies, advocates, and cheerleaders. *By listening fully and well, by making their associates feel valued, they accumulate a faithful following of people who promote and refer them in ways that advance their careers and help position them to accomplish even more!* And because good listeners are easy to talk to — they are often among the first to hear "insider information" about opportunities that advance their careers. Another bonus for good listeners is that because they make other people feel important, they are kept in mind for company social events to entertain clients or prospects. Their success as listeners makes them come to mind for meetings and gatherings that others simply don't have access to.

And the listener benefits from the process in other ways, too — perhaps in an even more meaningful way. In *Mission Possible* (McGraw-Hill, 1997), Ken Blanchard points out that "When we truly listen to another, it not only brings out their magnificence, it does the same for us." Intently focused listening is a priceless gift, and when we give something of such great value to others, we replenish our own reserves and rekindle our own spirits. Think of how revitalized you felt after you did some meaningful community service that made a differ-ence in someone's life. The same is true for total listening — you receive as well as give. And the positive experience energizes you to accomplish even more!

2. Good listeners have fewer interpersonal conflicts.

Because good listeners also use their skills outside the office, they tend to have fewer interpersonal conflicts with family, neighbors or friends to distract them and drain their energy. We've all had non-work related concerns that we slipped into our briefcases right along with that important proposal we were working on. When our minds and hearts are occupied with disturbing thoughts and worries, we are disconnected from the work we are trying to accomplish. Our cognitive processes become diffuse and fragmented when we try to resolve a conflict and accomplish a task at the same time. We can't do either well. The energy drain of miscommunication from ineffective listening undermines our productivity and ultimately our long-term success.

But when our intellectual and emotional energy are fully available to us, we are capable of "flow," the experience of being so fully engaged in an endeavor that we are unaware of the passage of time. We become so absorbed that we work effortlessly with total focus, oblivious to what is going on around us. During times of "flow" we become so proficient — so charged — that we rise to the realm of peak performance. Instead of feeling fatigued by the challenge of the work, we feel energized, refreshed, replenished. There is such inherent joy and satisfaction in the process that the usual struggle is replaced with feelings of competence and ease. What we are attempting to do takes on a life of its own and soars. Our accomplishment skyrockets!

The toll of interpersonal conflict generated by ineffective listening diminishes our likelihood of achieving "flow." The boundless energy of flow is short-circuited by replaying the recent friction. According to Daniel Goleman, author of *Emotional Intelligence* (Bantam, 1995), our brains operate less efficiently when we are worried and our concentration strained. He explains that intense concentration is one way to enter flow but that ". . . it takes considerable effort to get calm and focused enough to begin the task . . . ." Bottom line: *When we minimize the stress in our lives — and one way to do that is to listen well — we maximize our chances to achieve "flow," the mental state that affords us the greatest opportunity for accomplishment and success.*

3 Good listeners make fewer mistakes.

We've all witnessed or participated in some variation of the following scenario:

The boss calls a meeting to provide background and distribute assignments for an exciting new project. Team members are appraised of their tasks and deadlines. The urgency of completing all portions on time is emphasized. A week later when the team reconvenes to assemble the project, two people are behind schedule. One said he thought that a rough — not a final — draft was due. The other had the wrong date.

In addition to costing their organization money for express service at the photographer, printer, and post office, the team members who didn't listen effectively lost something much more valuable — their aura of competence. When the boss needs someone to delegate an important job to, the people who performed well last time will come to mind, not the team players who misunderstood. When there's an opening at the next level, guess who will move up the ladder? *When we make sure we receive information accurately, we make fewer time-consuming and costly mistakes that impede our progress toward accomplishing our goals.*

When the situation calls for hearing and understanding information about the delivery of a product or service, good listeners shine. Customers love them because they deliver accurately and on time And if they "hear" urgency in a customer's voice, they go out of their way to make sure the order is processed quickly and correctly, and they are rewarded with repeat business. Their bosses love them because they make them look good when they make quotas. It's not hard to figure out whose star is rising to sales manager strata.

How to Become an "Accomplished" Listener

While some people seem to have a natural gift for listening, anyone with a positive attitude and a willingness to learn can become an excellent listener. Listening is a set of skills that can be taught, learned, practiced, mastered. The following listening strategies will help you become a more effective listener who will ultimately accomplish more in life!

1. Listen longer than is necessary.

Have you ever visited your doctor, lawyer, or other practitioner and found yourself in the parking lot afterwards thinking about the questions you didn't ask? Maybe you felt the person was rushed and you made a decision not to "impose." Worse yet, the obvious time constraint raised your anxiety to the point that you didn't even remember the questions until later. It will probably take two phone calls to remedy the situation — your message to the office and the return call to you. If this becomes a pattern, you may seek care or service elsewhere. The dissatisfaction we experience when we are not really listened to is profound. And the inefficiency it creates lowers productivity and morale.

When we exhibit "listening readiness" behaviors such as extended time and pauses, the speaker recognizes instantly that we are serious about listening. The exchange now has the potential for maximum impact, whether it is to share information or air a concern.

Try these two closely-related techniques to convey your willingness to listen longer than is necessary:

Extend your listening time.

The realities of contemporary life dictate that we do things in a hurry. Multiple roles, deadlines, and the do-more-with-less mentality push us to accelerate our lives to the speed of urgency. This fast-forward lifestyle is a setup for communication disasters.

The technology that supports multi-tasking — call interruption, instant messages, cellular availability — condition us to accept rushing as a normal state of affairs. In everyday workplace communication we find ourselves busy preparing our response instead of listening. Or we become impatient and simply interrupt, leaving the speaker to feel annoyed or diminished. Given the enormous amount that we need to do, we feel our backs are to the wall and we have no choice but to barge into the conversation. But the benefits of slowing down while we listen far outweigh the perceived "inconvenience." If we make the time, if we have the courage to linger long enough to truly listen, conversational miracles can occur.

When it appears that the speaker has finished, simply wait a few seconds — try three — before responding to indicate that you are still in "listening readiness" mode. When you respond prematurely you lose the potential to gain valuable information or to tip a conflict toward resolution. When you extend your listening time, positive and productive things happen:

- The speaker may spontaneously remember more information.

This is the "Oh, I almost forgot!" phenomenon, and it rarely occurs when the exchange feels rushed.

• The speaker may volunteer information s(he) was reluctant to offer earlier. Sometimes this involves admitting a mistake or making you aware of something you need to know. You now have the opportunity to correct a situation before it becomes more damaging or costly.

• The speaker feels valued as a source of information and regards you more favorably, setting the stage for constructive interaction in the future.

Pause before responding.

Speakers have long recognized the power of the pause to signal that something of importance is being said. The speaking pause says, "want to hear this." The long underrated listening pause says, "want to hear this." After you are confident that the speaker has finished, try pausing at least five or six seconds before responding. Initially, you will feel as if you are waiting for the seasons to change, but you will become accustomed to the silent pause. If you feel genuine discomfort, saying something like, "Just let me think a bit," will ease the situation. By creating space between the conversational stimulus and response, you transmit your intention to fully understand the message and its implications. And you reduce the possibility of costly and time-consuming miscommunication.

When you use the listening pause on a regular basis you will find that:

• If the circumstances are upsetting, you will remain calmer and better able to process information because your "strike-back" reaction diminishes. It's simply a variation of the "counting to ten" tool applied to the millennium workplace.

• The listener believes that you truly intend to understand the situation to the best of your ability.

• During a conflict, the speaker may shift toward compromise or come around to your point of view.

The essential difference between the lessening extension and the pause is the interval before speaking. The extension is approximately half the time as the pause. The first conveys a willingness to hear more while the second communicates that you are making a sincere effort to fully grasp the meaning before you react or respond.

In *How to Become a CEO* (Hyperion 1998), Jeffrey Fox observes that "Presidents reflect. They don't shoot from the hip. They think, consider, ponder, observe, probe and listen. They stop and observe. They stop before saying the wrong thing . . . . They stop before making a snap decision . . . . And they watch and listen some more." CEO's — accomplishers of the highest order — got where they are by a combination of traits and factors. Listening well ranks high among them.

2. Adapt your listening style to the situation.

When I studied to become a counselor, we spent many class hours discussing listening styles. Each of us has a preferred listening approach that influences how and what we hear. But continued use of our most comfortable style to the exclusion of others leads to costly miscommunication that affects morale, productivity, and profits. The key to effective listening is the flexibility to adapt our listening style to the continuously changing environments we encounter in today's workplace.

Truly skilled listeners don't have a single listening style — they have an entire repertoire. And they are adept at knowing which one best serves the situation and at discerning when to shift to a different modality. They use their ears to stay on their toes.

To determine which listening style is most appropriate to a specific situation, you need to know your goal. After you establish the purpose of your listening, you can select the correct mode to accommodate your intent as a listener. A style that works superbly well in one set of circumstances might actually be an obstacle to effective communication in a different arena.

There are excellent profiles available to help you determine your preferred listening style. These instruments reveal whether you are most comfortable in different realms — such as facts, feelings, or experiences. Each assessment tool has categories of listeners such as Empathic (or People-Oriented) and Informational (Or Content-Oriented). Most tools have four or five classifications of listening styles. In the absence of a profile, it's helpful to know some basics about the most frequently used listening styles.

• *Empathic listeners* hear the feelings behind the facts. When we share something significant with an empathic listener, we feel truly understood when they demonstrate that they have grasped the deeper impact of our revelation. If we tell them that a co-worker has stolen our idea, they not only hear the facts but also our feelings of betrayal and anger. They offer holistic responses that encompass both the mind and spirit. The empathic listener's goal is to provide non-judgmental support as the speaker expresses concerns.

• *Factual listeners* focus on content. These information-centered listeners are skilled at identifying the critical facts in a conversation. They have a natural aptitude for determining the central issue and the details that support it. During a meeting or presentation, they ask questions and request clarification until they fully understand. They take detailed notes, especially in new situations. Their goal is to obtain accurate information, and they will pursue a topic diligently until they feel completely comfortable with their knowledge of it.

• *Judgmental listeners* evaluate the content of the message relative to their own frame of reference. They would have done well on the debate team because they are skilled in gathering facts and using them to reach a conclusion or prepare a rebuttal. They are not widely known for neutrality and will ultimately accept or reject a message. Their listening goal is to make the best decision with the information available and with their own opinions. Once they have weighed their options, they are determined and decisive. Attentive listeners genuinely relish hearing a story, anecdote or presentation. Attentives generally participate in discussions, reflect positive energy, and send signals that they like your message. They make excellent audiences because they are experience-oriented, and they notice all the details you spent your time and energy developing. Their goal is to thoroughly enjoy the time they spend listening.

The challenge is to know which style to use when!

A person in the middle of relating an exciting vacation experience appreciates an Attentive listener and would be put off by a Factual's repeated requests for details. Someone who spent two months on a proposal only to have it rejected won't respond well to a Judgmental's well-intentioned advice for improving it. What he really needs is an Empathic who will respond first to his feelings of frustration and save the suggestions for later. Likewise, a supervisor with a pressing production problem doesn't need an Empathic's support as much as he needs a Factual's accurate information and possible solutions.

The key question to ask yourself is what will best serve the speaker at this moment. What is the goal of your listening? Try to get outside yourself and figure out what the speaker needs right now. Support? Information? A Good Audience? Advice? Even though you have a dominant listening style, you have the ability to understand the essentials of the other styles and you can tailor your response to the situation.

Good listeners tune in to the language within the language. They listen between the lines and respond accordingly. When they correctly discern which style works best for the situation, communication flows. When they are adept at switching modes as circumstances dictate, they orchestrate seamless transitions from one person or task to another

• If Empathic listening seems to be the best choice, hold all solutions until you have adequately acknowledged the feeling. Be willing to discuss difficult topics even if doing so stretches your comfort zone a bit — you don't need to be a counselor, just a supportive listener. Look at the speaker and don't interrupt. Formulate your questions in an open-ended way. Instead of probing for a specific fact, ask for the speaker's reaction to the situation.

• If a Factual response is indicated, be precise and organized. Provide necessary details in a concise way without assumptions or speculation. Be logical and brief and offer evidence to support your conclusions. Don't offer unsupported opinions. Above all, be accurate. If you don't have an answer, don't even think about winging it. Find a place to get the right information and bring it back.

• If Attentive listening is appropriate, sit back and relax. Let the speaker tell the whole story and don't interrupt with a similar event that happened to you. Let the speaker have the spotlight while your body language — leaning forward a little, nodding — shows that you are appreciating his efforts. Even if the anecdote is about something you think is absurd, try to keep your inner critic silent and just go with the flow, unless the topic offends you.

• If Judgmental listening will work best, be prepared to back up your position with facts. Mentally prepare for some debate on the issue and remember that your best approach for this listening style is to be reasonable. Even though your judgment is being sought, you must establish your credibility. Keep your personal prejudices — and we all have them — out of play. Your role is to facilitate a thought process, not to persuade someone to your point of view.

Remember that flexible listening takes practice. To further your own learning, you can observe the conversations of others and decide which response style you think is best. Then listen to the interaction. What did the listener say? Was it a help or a hindrance? What might have worked better? The whole world is a laboratory for your listening practice.

3. Focus intently on tuning out distractions.

How do you react to someone who takes frequent call interruptions or reads E-mail (the telltale clicking is a giveaway) while on the phone with you? Probably the same way you respond to the person who looks over your shoulder while talking with you at a social event.

World class listeners focus on their subjects like laser beams. Because they demonstrate uncommon ability to tune out distractions, the speaker feels acknowledged and valued. When you give the gift of total, undivided attention to another person — and you don't even have to agree with what they are saying — you fulfill a basic human need to be noticed and heard. You create lifelong fans.

Two kinds of distractions — internal and external — compete with your ability to grasp the meaning of the message. Both are major deterrents to effective communication.

Internal distractors — creations of your own mind — sound like this: "So, what's he really trying to say?" "I wish she'd get to the point." "I wonder how late the dry cleaner is open." And "Boy, he likes to be the center of attention." These thoughts intrude on your ability to hear the speaker, and in many cases your facial expression and body language reveal your struggle to stay focused.

Internal distractors are like weeds — we get rid of them and they crop up again. It takes persistence and discipline to push them aside and concentrate on the message. Your sincere intent to do so is the secret to success. It's incredibly easy — and often fun---to entertain our own thoughts when we're supposed to be absorbed in someone else's. So we need to make a conscious choice to listen and when internal distractors encroach, push them back. Again and again. And on days when the struggle threatens to get the best of us, we can always ask the speaker to repeat a point and explain candidly that you're a little distracted.

External distractors relate to the environment — construction sounds, grass cutting, a noisy meeting in the next room. When conditions beyond your control compete with the speaker for your attention, try moving to a different room, maybe an empty office or conference room, long enough for the exchange. If possible, consider postponing the meeting until conditions are favorable for communication. Another more realistic option is to restructure your listening process. Tell the speaker you'll be asking for more clarification to offset the external stimuli.

Silence is More Than Golden

In The Spirit to Serve, Marriott's Way (Harper Business, 1997), J. W. Marriott observed that "after more than 40 years in business, I've concluded that listening is the single most important on-the-job skill that a good manager can cultivate. And the managers who practice this skill to perfection accomplish the most."

Maintaining total focus, selecting listening styles, listening for longer than is necessary: Mastering these three techniques will elevate your listening to a new level. When we listen well, our silence is more precious than gold. When we listen well we can better achieve our life purpose and support each other along the way. Try these strategies for 21 days — the time it generally takes to acquire new habits — and be prepared to watch your accomplishment quotient soar.

ABOUT
MAUREEN MURRAY, M.S. ED.

*M**aureen Murray is an author, speaker and trainer whose life work is helping people maintain perspective and communicate well. Her writing appears in newspapers and professional publications. In the past ten years she has enlightened hundreds of audiences with presentations on lowering stress and raising communication skills. Maureen holds masters' degrees from Duquesne University in Counseling and Educational Psychology. She draws on her mental health training to empower people to redesign their reaction to stress and to communicate from both the head and heart. Maureen is the author of "How to Sing in the Rain with a Frog in Your Throat", a collection of stories about how humor helps in difficult moments.*

Contact Information:
Maureen Murray
Humor Associates
225 Outlook Drive
Pittsburgh, PA 15228
phone: (412) 561-1577
fax: (412) 561-1559
e-mail: MMurrayHA@aol.com

STAY FIRED UP!
AND PREVENT BURNOUT

by Snowden McFall

Attention Achievers: Beware of Burnout

There is a fire inside you that ignites and burns brightly when you do what you love and you share that joy with others. As you accomplish more and more, living the life of your dreams, your contagious enthusiasm spreads from person to person. When you're Fired Up!, you can overcome any obstacle and succeed in ways that you never before thought possible. When you're Fired Up!, you have incredible energy and vitality, and you can continue to accomplish great things.[1]

But every once in a while, that fire starts to flicker and die, and what douses the flame is often burnout. All "doers" face the potential of burnout: overcommitting, doing too much, and losing your drive and energy. If you're Fired Up! about life and accomplish much on a regular basis, it's surprisingly easy for burnout to occur. It often starts out as a prolonged period of stress. Or it happens something like this:

You're working hard, balancing your family and your community obligations, and you're happy about your life. Because of the adage, "give a busy person something to do and it will get done," you are asked to take on another big responsibility. It might mean a raise or major growth for your company, so you say "yes." For a while, everything is fine. You're putting in more hours at work and getting less sleep, but you can handle it. Your fire is still stoked, although it begins to burn from both ends. And then your father is diagnosed with Alzheimer's. Emotionally distressed and guilt-ridden, you spend more time and money taking care of your father and less time taking care of yourself. Pretty soon, you're rushing around from place to place, feeling harried, worried about what you may have forgotten to do, and you fall into bed completely exhausted. You're eating poorly, just to have fuel in your body, snapping at loved ones and co-workers, dreading the next meeting. Your creativity and resourcefulness have vanished, and you have trouble getting up in the morning. You wonder how long you can go on like this. Your fire went out a long time ago, and you have no idea how to reignite the flame. This is the beginning of burnout.

It's an interesting phenomenon. Burnout rarely happens to procrastinators; it happens to doers. Doers live with a fair amount of stress anyway. Good stress occurs when we get excited about a new challenge. Bad stress occurs when a crisis or trauma takes place. Either way, it has a big impact on the central nervous system. Those of us who are already substantial achievers are the ones at the greatest risk. It takes very little to upset that delicate balance of easily juggling lots of different balls. All too quickly, added demands and pressure can force you into overload.

The Difference Between Burnout and Stress

All of us handle stress on a regular basis. It comes and goes depending on the demands of life. Certain events trigger serious stress: marriages, divorce, moving, changing careers, deaths of loved ones. Today, workplace stress contributes heavily to burnout. According to the the Center for Disease Control and Prevention, job stress is a major health threat. Forty percent of all workers rate their jobs as very or extremely stressful, and 25% say their jobs are the #1 one stressor in their lives. This kind of stress leads to illness and heart attacks.[2]

The Warning Signs of Burnout

You now know what contributes stress to your life. To ensure you control the stress and are not in danger of burning out, take a look at the two lists below. See which individual you identify with more strongly. Count how many statements are true for you.

Burnt-Out People:

- have no energy
- focus on the negative
- whine and complain frequently
- walk listlessly with their heads down
- don't take care of themselves
- eat poorly and rarely exercise
- rarely do what they love
- stay stuck in the past and are resistant to change
- are not fun to be around
- are ineffective at work
- criticize others frequently
- judge themselves especially harshly
- feel unappreciated
- take very little time with their personal appearance; look disheveled

Fired Up! People:

- have abundant energy
- focus on their wins and on good news
- speak enthusiastically
- walk with a spring in their step
- take care of themselves
- eat well and exercise regularly
- often do what they love
- focus on the present and welcome new ideas
- are great fun to be around
- light up the workplace with their good attitude
- laugh often
- continually work on themselves
- feel good about their work
- always look put together and polished; radiate a sense of well-being and health

How did you do? Do you have five or more symptoms? If so, relax and take a deep breath. Help is on the way. The next several pages will give you practical hands-on tips that really work to reignite your fire and help you shift into a positive, proactive healthy state. Even if you've tried them before, approach the ideas with a fresh perspective. You're in a different place from where you've ever been before.

What to Do When You're Burnt-Out

Spark #1 — Take Control of Something Small

Often when we're very stressed, we feel out of control. Remedy the situation by taking control of something small and manageable. If your desk is totally cluttered and can be tackled in a few hours, do it. If you feel like washing the kitchen floor, go for it. Experience the completion of that activity. Choose an activity that's quick and easy, so you can feel a sense of satisfaction and can see the fruits of your labor. Completion releases its own special energy, so pick something you know you can get done in a few hours. Then complete it. That will at least get you back into a more positive frame of mind, and let you know that you do get things done, even if you're not feeling that way now.

Spark # 2 — Go On Vacation

The most immediate "quick fix" for burnout is to schedule a vacation as soon as possible and go away for at least a week. Ten days is better if you can manage it. You need to get away from all the stressful pressures around you, and you need to relax in a peaceful setting where your only responsibilities are to rest and take care of yourself. If money is tight, ask a friend if you can stay in his vacation home. If you have to take time off without pay, do so. You are in desperate need of a break. I know this from personal experience.

Two years into my business, thanks to heavy stress in my life, my blood sugar dropped dramatically. I felt faint and dizzy. I went to see my doctor and he diagnosed me as hypoglycemic. He also gave me some very good advice. In my line of work, owning a a high-pressure ad agency and professional speaking business, I needed to take a minimum of two full weeks off every year. He said as soon as I got back from one vacation, I should schedule the next one. Since then, I've taken that advice to heart. As a 16-year entrepreneur and author with three businesses, I take four weeks of vacation with my husband every year. It keeps both of us fresh and Fired Up! We love our lives and our work, but we can't do it 365 days. We know this time off is critical to our effectiveness at work. We always get out of the house, because vacations at home are not vacations. We usually go sailing in the Virgin Islands. Our biggest decisions are where to dine each night and what novel to read next. It's heaven and it works.

If for some reason, you cannot get away immediately for a vacation, take a couple of days off and take day trips to someplace soothing in nature. Go to the ocean or the mountains; spend some time outdoors, whether you're hiking or just sitting quietly by a lake. The key is downtime away from home in a safe place. No hassles, no decisions — just relaxation. Ask a family member to take care of the kids and find a way to do it. *It's extremely important.*

Spark #3 — Track Your Successes Daily

Get yourself an attractive journal. Then every night, before you go to bed, write down your successes from that day. Each of us accomplishes so much, but when you're burning out, you may not realize it. The very first success may be "Got out of bed" because you did, even when you didn't want to. "Got the kids to school" might be number 2, and so on. Give yourself credit for every phone call, every meeting, every report, every e-mail. Burnt-out people feel like they don't get anything done, and that simply is not true. Try this technique for a month. I guarantee it will boost your self-esteem. And just imagine how you'll feel if you do it for a whole year. I've been doing this off and on for over a decade, and it makes a huge difference in my life. It helps me lighten up and rekindle my fire. It's even more important to do when I'm terribly busy, because otherwise I can't keep track of it all.

Spark #4 — Just Say No

When your embers are dying, one of the best things you can do is say "no." That means "no" to anything new, "no" to any additional tasks or responsibilities, "no" to any social events that mean work for you. Get yourself in balance, and cut back on your overtaxed life. Stop doing so many things. Don't agree to help everyone else. Take care of yourself first. You're worth nothing to anyone else if you are exhausted and demoralized. You owe it to yourself and to others to say "no" while you recharge. There are huge payoffs when you simplify your life. Try it.

Spark #5 — Ask for Help

You cannot possibly do everything. And during stressful periods, you cannot function at peak performance. Ask for help. Level with the people in your life, at home and at work. Tell them you're going through a tough time, and you need their support. Delegate more to your co-workers and employees, ask for their advice and input, get some fresh ideas. Don't try to do everything yourself. Even consider adding short-term staffing, like a temp, to do administrative tasks. Ask others to help you and give them permission to do the same when they're stressed. There's nothing to be ashamed of by reaching out; we are all human beings, not human "doings." We all go through tough periods, and we are much more respected when we admit our vulnerability and express our needs. You may be astonished at the support that comes your way. And if you don't feel comfortable sharing at work, go to a support group or therapist. The key is to unburden and get help.

Spark #6 — Stop Doing and Start Being

This is one of the most challenging mandates for a doer in the throes of burn-out. But it is also one of the most healing. Stop doing and start being. Start honoring yourself as a worthwhile individual regardless of what you accomplish in the world. Go inside yourself and discover who you really are. Consider going to a spa or meditation retreat. Take yoga or Tai-chi. Do something that will help you go inside to discover who you really are in the silence. Most of us are not aware that we are all divine beings, with access to limitless creativity and resources, if only we would ask.

Whatever your source of spiritual inspiration, whether you believe in God, Buddha, Mohammed, Christ or just love, spend some time developing that part of yourself. Pray, meditate, chant, or just be quiet and write what guidance you receive. Many of the world's great achievers have turned inside to discover deeper meaning and purpose in their lives. The outside world is ephemeral; success and outer accolades are fleeting. But the inside core of who you are is solid and good, whole and complete, all by itself. Few of us truly know this, inside of ourselves. Achievers do so frequently out of a need to have the rest of the world tell them they are OK. Learn to validate yourself from the inside out and discover what an incredible difference it makes in your life.

Many gifts will come from this experience. You'll no longer be dependent on the praise of others. You'll be more confident and grounded because you'll come from a deeper place of wisdom and knowing. Today's little dilemmas won't throw you off balance, because you'll recognize that in the grand scheme of things, very little of today's nonsense matters. But most of all, you'll discover an ocean of peace and fulfillment that can renew you each day, if you take the time to go there. It's up to you. The rewards are infinite.

Spark #7 — Play Like a Child

There's a reason that young children are so happy most of the time. They play often. They live totally in the present moment and are not worried about tomorrow. They continually feed and express their imagination by using all of their senses and experimenting. That's why play is the perfect antidote to the stress of burnout. Why do you think golf is so popular? People get outdoors in nature, laugh and play.

Spend some time thinking about what you consider fun. You'll probably discover that you haven't spent much time having fun lately. Pick three favorite activities and schedule them next week. Now do another one in the next eight hours. Then go do it. If you don't have many activities that you consider to be play, it's time to cultivate some new hobbies. Consider taking a class, trying something new, playing with your children.

My husband and I have developed an eclectic list of interests. We might be working on our dollhouse, riding our tandem bicycle, going sailing or skiing, taking a ballroom dancing class, critiquing the latest movie, shopping, dining out, entertaining friends, or reading the new bestseller. We are continually trying new things and introducing each other to new activities. This keeps us both energized and Fired Up!

Spark #8 — Focus on Good News and Avoid Negative People

Dr. Martin Sullivan of the University of Pennsylvania discovered that, after 20 years of research interviewing 350,000 executives, the top 10% performers think differently from others; they all have the quality of optimism.

It's also been documented that we have at least 50,000 thoughts a day, and that for most people, 75%-85% are negative. When you're in danger of burnout, you need to change your internal programming and focus on positive, powerful thoughts which get you Fired Up! and help you maintain your optimism.

We live in a negative society which focuses on negative news. Every workplace has an "ain't it awful" club whining about the bad news and stirring up trouble. Avoid this group. Stay away from gossips and naysayers. Avoid negative family members when you're under stress. You may even need to avoid your parents.

At work, counteract the negativity by sharing good news. Ask your employees and family every few days, what's the good news? Cultivate optimism and you'll start yourself back on track. *Take a lesson from actor Christopher Reeve, who believes that keeping your negativity to yourself is a way of taking control of your life.*

Spark #9 — Spend Time Helping Someone Less Fortunate

In my experience, this is the single most powerful antidote to stress and burnout other than a vacation. No matter how bad your life is, no matter what's wrong, there is always someone who has it worse. Always. So pick yourself up and do something about it. Even something as simple as babysitting the neighboring single mom's kids so she can go to the grocery store will do wonders for your well-being.

Get out of your self and serve other people. The treasure of service is that it gives you just as much as the people you serve. Find some way to give back. And when you're feeling sorry for yourself, do a reality check. Do you still have your limbs, your senses? Do you have shelter and food? Is there anyone in your life who loves you? Then you're better off than lots of people.

Spark #10 — Set Boundaries

People who give a great deal are often unclear about their boundaries. In addition to saying "no" more often, make your boundaries clear with others. It can be as simple as telling others, " You know, I hate to be criticized," or "I'm leaving the room before this becomes a fight." Learning how to prevent escalating friction can dramatically lower stress levels. When one of us knows that we're in a bad mood at the office, we warn everyone else. That way, others know to tread lightly and bring up touchy subjects at another time.

Spark #11 — Forgiveness

All of us are human and we get hurt. Sometimes people do absolutely awful things to us, and we find it hard to forgive them. A recent Gallup poll on death found that those adults who had not a chance to say goodbye to their loved ones or make peace were experiencing stress. Fifty-six percent of all adults were afraid they wouldn't be forgiven by God.

My experience is that God forgives everything. And that incredible liberation comes from forgiving someone who has hurt you. The amazing thing is that forgiveness is not for them; it's for you. As long as some part of your consciousness is tied up in righteousness about how wrong and awful they were, a part of you lives under stress and is not accessible for creativity. You hurt yourself when you hold onto the past. Let it go, forgive, and observe the newfound freedom you experience. You won't know this until you try it. But it can relieve more stress than a massage.

Spark #12 — Pamper Yourself

When you're on the verge of burnout, pampering yourself can be the perfect antidote. Take a warm bubble bath with candles and your favorite music. Eat your favorite foods. Get a massage, manicure, or pedicure. Let someone do something for you, for a change. Nurture yourself both on the inside and out. Eat healthy, nutritious foods that make your skin glow. Buy a new outfit that makes you feel like a million bucks (don't spend a million on it, however!). Do the little things that make you feel special and loved.

How to Stay Fired Up! for Life

Now you know what to do when you're in danger of burning out. Here's a quick list of actions to take to stay Fired Up! throughout your life.

- Take time to re-evaluate your life every so often. Are you on track, are you living your dreams, are you enjoying your work?
- Take courses in things that are of interest to you — lifelong learning keeps you healthy and happy.
- Learn from your mistakes. Don't expect yourself to be perfect.

- Do work that really fulfills you and is aligned with your life purpose.
- Exercise often to relieve stress and get healthy. Pick something you really enjoy and can do anywhere.
- Have a good time-management system and use it religiously.
- Get enough sleep. Few Americans get the eight plus hours they need to prevent accidents and injuries on the job or while driving.[4]
- Laugh often. It heals illnesses and keeps you energized. Watch funny movies, listen to funny audiotapes, go to comedy clubs.
- Remember that people are what's truly important. Love others and yourself.
- Do something every day that you absolutely love to do.
- Have an attitude of gratitude. Maintain a gratitude journal.
- Recognize that the Golden Rule applies to everything. You get back what you send out.
- Praise others publicly; give recognition regularly.
- Focus on your wins. Have a victory wall.
- Celebrate life's special moments.
- Take good care of yourself and your loved ones.

Keep Your Fire Burning

We've covered lots of territory in this chapter. You now know the key causes of your stress, the warning signals for burnout, and how to remedy severe stress if it shows up. You have all the matches, kindling, and sparks to ignite your fire and set it ablaze. You are already a doer - someone who accomplishes much in your life. Take the next step and be a healthy doer, one who takes care of yourself, keeps your stress levels low, and stays Fired Up! You have great gifts inside you, and the world will be a poorer place if you don't share them. Ignite your flame and share your gifts with the world. The time is now. The choice is yours. Ignite your fire and stay Fired Up!

Footnotes:

1. McFall, Snowden, *Fired Up! How to Succeed by Making Your Dreams Come True*. North Bridge Press, 1998.

2. Winik, Lyric Wallwork, "Let Go of Stress," *Parade Magazine*, July 11, 1999, p. 4-6.

3. *Self Magazine*, July 1998.

4. William Dement, "Snooze Alarm", *People Magazine*, October 4, 1999, p. 147-149.

ABOUT
SNOWDEN MCFALL

Snowden McFall, author, trainer and speaker, is President of Brightwork Advertising and Training, founded in 1983. She was named the National Women in Business Advocate of the Year by the Small Business Administration (SBA) for helping female entrepreneurs. She was chosen as a finalist for Inc. *Magazine's New England Entrepreneur of the Year Award. A graduate of Vassar College with a master's degree from Brown University, she is the author of "Fired Up! How to Succeed by Making Your Dreams Come True" and "Let's Get Fired Up!" Snowden has appeared on over 300 radio stations and was recently featured on CNN, the Home Shopping Network and Bloomberg Television.*

Contact Information:
Snowden McFall
Brightwork Advertising and Training
74 Northeastern Blvd., Unit 20
Nashua, NH 03062
phone: (888) FIREBKS
phone: (603) 882-0600
e-mail: SMcFall@FiredUp-TakeAction-Now.com
web: www.FiredUp-TakeAction-Now.com

Creating Tomorrow's Opportunities Out of Today's Changes

by Barbara Mintzer

Employees today have very definite ideas of what they want and expect from a job and the company they work for. A few generations ago "a good day's pay for a good day's wage" was sufficient to keep many people on the job for a long time. If you threw in benefits too, most people would stay FOREVER. That is not the case today. Today's employee comes into a company with the mindset of "you should be grateful to have me here, and this is what I want." They have a sense of *entitlement* not seen in employees before, and managers and supervisors are dealing with the challenge of motivating these very independent, free-thinking people to buy into the corporate vision.

Being a business leader today requires the ability to implement two styles of management that are new to the corporate environment. These two styles, used during different stages of organizational change, are *the visionary* and *the coach*. These management styles are far removed from the more structured and formal hierarchical style usually implemented in business.

The visionary has the challenge of formulating and articulating a corporate vision that the employees can buy into and work towards.

What drives this style is the conviction, passion and enthusiasm the leader has in both the formulation and articulation of this vision. Most employees will not buy into a vision unless they believe in and trust the leader and can feel the leader's own enthusiastic excitement. When organizational change is rampant in a company, and people feel their sense of control and security being taken away, *why should they stay?* What is in it for them in the long run? That is where the visionary comes in. The visionary has the ability to help people see the light at the end of the tunnel . . . and what a great light it is going to be! The visionary can aim big and bring everyone along for the journey, making each person responsible for his or her part in seeing that the vision becomes a reality.

However, before you can formulate a vision for people to follow, you must determine what your *values* are. Your corporate vision will be a direct reflection of your corporate values. The following is the VALUES STATEMENT of the Sierra Vista Regional Medical Center in San Luis Obispo, CA.; however, the values expressed in this statement hold true for any industry.

Sierra Vista Regional Medical Center
Values Statement

Demonstrate Respect

We believe each person is a unique expression and therefore inherently valuable.

We believe every encounter is an opportunity to respond to unique individual needs.

We focus on the care we provide to patients, treating them with dignity, respect and compassion.

We acknowledge the unique gifts and diversity of our physicians and employees and seek to integrate those talents in an atmosphere of mutual respect.

We are accountable to the organization, to our patients and to each other.

Foster Integrity

We believe truth and honesty guide our thoughts and our actions at all times.

We are individually responsible for what we do and say.

We build relationships based on trust.

We act ethically in all interactions — there should be no undue influences, conflicts of interest or biased judgments affecting our decision making.

We create an environment that promotes the open and honest exchange of ideas.

Embrace Change

We believe innovation and change must be welcomed and nurtured in order for our organization to increase its capacity to learn and progress.

We encourage the development of a questioning mindset . . . new ways of thinking about everything we do.

We strive to be a learning organization that promotes continuous learning, cultivates creativity and rewards innovation and risk-taking.

We are committed to being flexible and continually responsive to changes in the environment.

We push on the existing boundaries and challenge ourselves to exceed our own expectations and those of others.

Enhance Value

We focus all our efforts on meeting the needs of our patients, physicians, employees, shareholders, communities and others whom we serve.

We ensure quality and cost effectiveness, which are not incompatible, but rather interdependent concepts.

We expect accountability for excellence in performance and for adherence to professional and organizational standards.

We create a work environment that helps people realize their full potential.

We believe economic security for our employees and our physician partners comes from being part of a successful organization.

We bring value to shareholders through effective stewardship of resources, including effective management of corporate expense.

We constantly search for productivity and process improvement consistent with our commitment to quality.

We monitor and evaluate our delivery of care, our business operations and our organizational climate to ensure they meet the needs of those we serve.

We work with others to deliver quality care in our communities and to promote overall community growth and success.

Lead Through Partnership

We lead with our partners to build strategic alliances in order to effectively meet our communities' and nation's healthcare needs.

We recognize that individual, institutional and societal interests are often in tension; we are committed to being an advocate for what is right recognizing that in every case we must discern how the good of the whole can be served.

We seek to establish mutually beneficial and accountable partnerships based on shared values.

We are dedicated to working for a health system that is accessible and affordable to all.

We join with our physicians and other healthcare organizations to form cost effective care networks focused on quality and responsive to the needs of employers and other purchasers.

The above VALUES STATEMENT is used with permission of the Sierra Vista Medical Center, San Luis, Obispo, CA.

What a terrific VALUES STATEMENT that is. Out of that can come *your* Vision Statement.

Vision Statement

We are the provider of choice for our products and services.

We are a company that demonstrates respect to customers, clients, and each other. Everyone is responsible for his or her actions, and all who work here are committed to embracing change. We focus all our efforts on enhancing the value of the service we bring to our customers, and we build strategic alliances in our community and industry to meet our customers' needs.

That could be your Vision Statement. It is clear, concise, and has enough in it so that every employee can find something he or she could do to bring your vision into fruition. You may want a Vision Statement that has more measurable and quantifiable elements to it. Your Vision Statement could be: We are the company of choice for our line of products and services, and we realize a 20 percent increase in revenue each year, or a 10 percent increase in our client base. However you choose to word your Vision Statement, you are giving your employees the "framework" by which they can see themselves involved in making that vision a reality. Once your employees buy into your Vision Statement, they will immediately start to think about ways they can help you achieve it.

Why is it so important for leaders and employees alike to have a vision?

• Having a vision helps us structure our lives according to our priorities.

We all have such full plates today that it is difficult to know what to do first. However, when you have a vision of what you want to achieve, and you can "taste" what it would be like to achieve it, you start to gravitate to those activities and projects that will lead you closer to your vision. You get that little "quirk" in your heart when you have done something that directly relates to what you are trying to accomplish, and you get that feeling in the pit of your stomach when you are working on something that you know will not lead you where you need to go. The vision we hold becomes the compass that keeps us on track. I find when I am working towards my vision, I somehow still have the time to take care of the day-to-day business that must also get done. It seems my energy level is the highest when I am in gear and motivated to achieve my vision. Many business leaders have told me that a worthy goal or vision is the "fire in the belly" that keeps them going.

- Having a vision help us become failure-resistant.

When I first started speaking, it was a means to get clients for my practice as a career and life-plannning specialist. I would speak to any group that asked, usually breakfast and luncheon talks to local clubs and associations in my city. I spoke for two years and never got paid, and at first never thought about speaking as a profession. But I found after two years that I was enjoying the speaking more than the counseling. The dynamics of a group, and me in front of the group motivating many people instead of counseling one, was much more satisfying to me. I had just finished my second year of free speeches, when a gentleman asked me to speak for a group he belonged to and asked, "What is your fee?" I almost fainted; I had never heard that before . . . someone thought my speaking was worthy of a fee. While my fee was certainly low (I had no idea what to charge) I WAS A PAID SPEAKER!!! That fee and the fact that someone paid me to speak gave me the courage and the validity I needed to pursue my career as a professional speaker. From that moment on (17 years ago) *I could not walk into a room without visualizing myself in front of an audience speaking and having an impact on the lives of the people in my audience.* In those 17 years I have had my ups and downs, my successes and failures, but the vision has never left me. I may make mistakes and fail to live up to my own high expectations of myself, but

I am not a failure. I can't allow failure and my vision of me into my life at the same time. As long as I stay true to my vision and work towards it, I know it will keep me failure-resistant.

• Having a vision gives us a common bond and purpose to strive for.

One of the most important facets of a vision is the power it has to unify people to strive towards a common goal. When a corporate vision becomes more important than an individual's personal agenda, you rise above the "turf" issues and power struggles that can happen at work. Especially during times of organizational change, it is crucial that everyone has a "shared vision" of what the company seeks to accomplish and what his or her part is in it.

• Having a vision gives purpose and meaning to life.

A vision is the structure that gives life its meaning and purpose. A vision gives us the reason to stretch ourselves, get out of our comfort zones and try something new . . . a reason not only to embrace change but initiate it. Even though change may be unsettling, if there is something we want to be, do, or have, we will usually bite the bullet and go after it. We learn to look at change as a friend, not as an enemy. A vision allows us a view of what we can aspire to if we are willing to do the work and make it happen.

Many managers and supervisors have told me that while the above sounds wonderful, they have had challenges in getting their employees to "buy into" the corporate vision. It has been my experience in working with so many companies that when employees don't buy into a vision, it is because they feel their work would have little impact on the vision so why bother anyway.

They do not feel *accountable* for the vision, and that must change. It is the leader's responsibility to make employees accountable for their contribution to the vision.

The following is a *very specific, very powerful* strategy to use to give your employees buy-in and make them accountable for the vision. However, this strategy will work only if it is followed exactly as I present it here.

You have now formulated a vision for your employees to work towards. What follows is the *15-minute vision meeting.*

Let us say, hypothetically, every Friday morning you and your staff meet from 9:00 til 9:15. Every Friday you meet at the same time, in the same room, everyone takes the same seat, and you always ask the same two questions of your staff:

1. What did you do that brought us closer to our vision?

2. What obstacles did you encounter that prevented you from getting us closer to our vision?

That is it! Those two questions never change; they are the same two questions asked week after week, always on the same day (Friday) same time (9:00 to 9:15) in the same room with everyone sitting in the same seat week after week. The power of this strategy lies in the fact that nothing changes. It takes about three months for your staff to build a "vision mentality," but after three months that Friday meeting is imbedded in their routine. So now it is Wednesday, and one of your employees is thinking, "Oh boy, it's Wednesday . . . in two days I'm going to be asked those same two questions again. *I had better come up with something to bring us closer to the vision.*" You will be amazed at what that employee will give you.

I have had managers and supervisors write to me telling me that they really did not know if the 15-minute vision meeting would work, but they were willing to give it a try. And they told me what I have just told you . . . after about three months they started to get some of the most creative and innovative ideas from their employees . . . and they said they got some of the best ideas from the people they expected the least of. *Give your employees accountability and encourage and support their willingness to give you ideas, and they can move your company ahead in quantum leaps.*

Once your employees are actively supporting your corporate vision and working towards making it a reality, the management style of coaching is the most effective way you can sustain employee productivity and effectiveness. This hands-on, one-of-the-team style of management provides a climate of trust that is conducive to keeping employees motivated and engaged in their work. There are four key qualities to effective coaching:

1. Loyalty: Employees today do not feel much loyalty from management. They have seen family and friends go through layoffs in recent years, and they come into the workplace with a self-protective attitude. It is *imperative* that management show loyalty to employees for a coaching relationship to work. While companies may no longer be able to guarantee "forever" employment, coaches can show loyalty to their employees in a number of ways:

• Honest communication . . . give timely and reliable information to your employees . . . always important, and especially so when an organization is going through change. If they trust you and respect you and know you are being honest with them, they will be able to handle the information even if it is not positive. Most employees will give you everything they have to help you turn the situation around if they feel included.

• Allow employees to express how they feel without fear of punishment or retribution . . . a must if you want to build trust and loyalty with your staff.

• Never ask employees to do something that goes against company ethics or values.

• Encourage employees to grow and develop their potential, and support them in their endeavors. Be grateful for the risk-takers in your organization; it's their creativity and innovative thinking that will keep your company competitive. Encourage and support risk-taking, provided the ideas and actions are thought-out beforehand and are not reckless.

• Treat each employee as a unique individual. Everyone wants to be appreciated and acknowledged for his or her own special attributes. Get to know your employees better so you know their frustrations as well as their aspirations. The most effective coach is the one who is truly "tuned in" to the players on his or her team.

2. Empathetic Listening: One of the most undervalued of all management skills is the ability to listen. A coach often spends more time listening than managing. When an employee needs to be heard, the coach:

• Finds a private spot (a neutral place like the cafeteria off-hours if the employee is likely to feel intimidated in the coach's office) and makes time available to listen.

• Holds all calls unless urgent and lets the employee know that there will be absolutely no interruptions. The employee has all the coach's time for (x) amount of minutes. We spend time with things we value, and this non-interrupted time is a strong signal to the employee that he or she is important and valued.

• Sits down and leans forward in an "I am interested" position and focuses on what the employee is saying, sometimes taking notes if appropriate.

• Asks open-ended questions to draw the employee out and pays close attention to what is said. Try asking questions such as: What are your persistent frustrations? What do you need to perform your job that has not been provided? What would the ideal job in this company look like for you? In the answers to these questions you discover what is at the heart of the problem, and your employee will feel understood when his or her needs and concerns can be accurately verbalized by the coach.

• Lets the employee know that the coach is in his or her corner and willing to help. "How can *we* work through this?" is an excellent phrase for showing empathy and concern.

3. Skills Stretching: To run a team that is competitive, creative and innovative, the coach should create an environment in which employees are given an opportunity to develop new skills. Creative and innovative employees love to be challenged in their work and grow in new skill development. The coach should carefully evaluate the strengths,weaknesses, and confidence levels of each employee, and move individuals into areas where their skills can be expanded and their interests can be developed. Classes and seminars can be effective tools in achieving skills-stretching. However, sometimes all it takes to develop potential is added responsibility and encouragement along the way.

4. Role Modeling: Coaches are role models whether they know it or not. The staff members' view of the coach can affect their attitude towards the entire organization. How each staff member feels about the coach can have a profound effect on how productive he or she is. Coaches can be excellent role models by:

• Providing a "level playing field." The coach does not show favoritism, and each employee is judged equally on his or her work performance.

• Giving employees constant and consistent feedback on their performance.

• Showing appreciation for employees. When coaches give employees approval, praise, and recognition when it is due, employees respond by becoming more committed to the company and to the vision it aspires to.

• Taking pride in themselves and their own work and emulating the behavior that they would require of their employees.

Coaching is not easy. But the reward is great . . . a cohesive, alive, "excited about the future" team working together towards a shared vision. It is this type of team that will keep a company competitive and on top in this rapidly changing workplace.

ABOUT
BARBARA MINTZER

*B*arbara Mintzer is an internationally recognized, award-winning speaker with over 25 years in business. She was one of the first women in the United States to sell wholesale pharmaceuticals for a major drug company. Her ability to create selling opportunities where none previously existed earned her numerous honors, including a cover story in the American Druggist *magazine. After successfully moving up into management, Barbara moved on, and in 1982, formed her own consulting and training company. Barbara specializes in helping organizations, teams and individuals create tomorrow's opportunities out of today's changes. More than 80,000 business and healthcare professionals from the United States, Canada, England, Australia and Brazil have benefited from her rich blend of humor and personal insights to create a powerful and inspiring message.*

Contact Information:
Barbara Mintzer
B.A. Mintzer & Associates
4019A Otono Drive
Santa Barbara, CA 93110
phone: (800) 845-3211
phone: (805) 964-7546
fax: (805) 964-9636
e-mail: bmintzer@west.net
web: www.Speaking.com/Mintzer.html

REROUTING YOUR CHILDHOOD ROOTS TO ACCOMPLISH MORE IN YOUR LIFE

by Christina Bergenholtz, M.Ed.

D
o you ever ask yourself, "What's holding me back from accomplishing what I really want to do in life?" I recall many frustrating moments when I worked in corporate America and also after I started my own speaking and training business when I would ponder such questions. Why wasn't I accomplishing things faster? How long was it going to take to get this business off the ground? What is holding me back from moving forward? I once taught a workshop in which I was encouraging participants to find time to do things that were meaningful to them, yet I wasn't feeling fulfilled with all the activities I was pursuing.

Many people will agree that their parents or guardians had a major influence on their lives. I believe that our upbringing shapes who we are today. I lost my dad in May of 1995, and my mother died in May of the following year. I vividly recall my mother's words that last year of her life: "Chris, I am such a burden. You'll be so much better off once I'm gone. Then you'll finally be able to move forward with your life." While I was grieving the death of my parents, someone said to me: "You won't understand this now, but my life changed after my father died. He had always been a demanding person who made decisions for his kids, but after his death, I felt free to live my life the way I chose." Naturally, I couldn't relate to what he was saying. But shortly after that time I had a true "awakening." It all began with a dream I had one night.

In my dream my parents were taking a trip somewhere, and I was driving them to their destination. In the next scene, I watched as they walked hand in hand down a long, narrow corridor into a small, empty room. They had nothing with them, just each other. Suddenly, I felt sadness as my mother turned to my father and said, "Vincent, I'm so worried about the kids. I don't know what they'll do without us." In a calm, reassuring voice he replied, "Gladys, the kids will be OK. It's time for us to go."

My dream then took me to a large gymnasium, in the center of which was an enormous yellow balloon that filled almost the entire gym. I stood on the sidelines, as I had done many times in my life, looking up at the balloon and wondering why it was there. And then I saw myself sitting on top of it. I was grasping the balloon with both hands as it swayed back and forth. The part of me that was watching from the sidelines felt tremendous fear and yelled, "Hold on! Hold on! You won't fall!" The part of me that was riding on the balloon, however, felt a sense of freedom and excitement.

I finally awakened from this dream, but I couldn't push it out of my mind. One week later, I was still thinking about it when I attended a workshop on how to organize your office presented by a woman named Ethel Cook. Each year Ethel proclaims one day in September as "Do It Day" when you clean out your office and get better organized. At the end of her workshop, she gave everyone a sticker. I gasped when I looked at the sticker, a yellow circle with the words "Do It Day!" imprinted on it. I was staring at the yellow balloon from my dream.

The important message in that dream then became clear to me: Let go of the past and move forward with my life — just do it. It was time to free myself from the obstacles that had been preventing me from being the person I am naturally and accomplishing the things that were truly meaningful to me.

The balloon in my dream represented a voyage on a hot-air balloon that would take me to interesting places. The color yellow signified the sun rising each day, bringing with it a new adventure or new knowledge about myself. The holding-on symbolized not only holding on for the excursion, but also letting go. In my dream, my parents didn't carry anything with them — the baggage wasn't included in their trip. This revealed that before I could ride that balloon to the fullest, I needed to let go of any excess baggage.

After discovering the excess baggage that was hindering my personal success, I was ready to move forward. Picture five pieces of luggage, each with a tag marked "unwanted labels," "old beliefs," "clutter," "uninspiring activities," and "fear." Once I released myself from each of these five pieces of baggage, I was free to begin my journey on the balloon.

Unwanted Labels

In my family, I was labeled the "quiet one." I can still hear my mother's words: "Oh, Chris, you were much too quiet when you were a kid. You would spend hours in your bedroom with the door closed, and sometimes I forgot that you were even there." Aargh! It's true that I often escaped to my bedroom to avoid family conflicts, and unlike my "talkative" sister, I kept everything to myself. As you can imagine, expectations aren't high when you're quiet. You don't get noticed, and frequently you don't ask for the things that you really want.

This label stayed with me into adulthood, and if someone asked me to describe myself, I would probably respond by saying that I was quiet by nature. Sometimes this quietness caused problems in the workplace. Fortunately, I was promoted many times, but that was due mostly to a strong work ethic (which you will read about later). But I didn't always get the positions I wanted, the raise I thought I deserved, or the resources I needed because I wasn't used to asking for what I wanted.

The dream helped me to realize that I hate that label. Once I freed myself from being the "quiet one," I started to see myself differently. Sometimes people are even surprised when I tell them the story I just shared. After all, in my business as a speaker, educator, and consultant, I spend lots of time talking. But there are times when I do like being quiet; however, I prefer to describe myself as reflective. As a reflective person, I have chosen writing as an exciting adventure in learning about myself and enhancing my business.

Now it's your turn to think about unwanted labels. What label(s) would you like to leave behind?

How have these labels hindered you from accomplishing what you want in your personal life? In your professional life?

How can you turn those labels into something more positive?

Old Beliefs

When I was growing up, we didn't dare be too happy. Life was about working hard and occasionally experiencing some pleasures that would offer fleeting moments of joy. My father, who had a high school education, had worked as a laborer, a job he despised, for over 35 years. He certainly encouraged me to get an education so that I would have better job opportunities, but he defined a good job as working at a large company that provided security and impressive benefits for its employees.

My father used to get excited over the prospects of my working for the same company where he was employed. However, that never happened. Imagine my parents' dismay on the day when we all sat down and figured out that I had worked for 19 different companies by age 40. Neither of my parents believed in the concept of doing the kind of work you love. Needless to say, they could never understand why I didn't stay at one job longer than a couple of years. Because of their belief, I was successful at landing jobs in companies where people were basically unhappy, but I always had a driving force to find the job fulfillment that my father had never experienced.

When there is a voice in your head that repeats, "Work is work and it's not meant to be fun," it's difficult to convince yourself that you deserve to do the kind of work you really want. Once I released myself of my parents' beliefs, I experienced happiness to a greater degree and stopped feeling guilty about having a satisfying career. I can now comfortably say that I love my work. Plus, after taking a long-overdue trip to Scandinavia this past summer, I discovered that I also love to spend my earnings on things that are pleasurable, and I plan to travel regularly in the future.

What unrealistic beliefs are you still holding onto in your life? In your career?

Are these unrealistic beliefs preventing you from accomplishing what's important to you?

Are you ready to give them up for more positive beliefs that will help you (and others) move forward?

Clutter

After my parents died, my siblings and I sorted through their belongings. We held onto everything that was most precious to us and sold the rest at a large yard sale. At the time, I was convinced that I needed those precious items, and the spare room in my basement suddenly looked more like remnants from my parents' house. Many times my husband would ask me when I was planning to clean out that room, and each time I would tell him that I wasn't ready yet. The dream helped me to realize that I didn't need those things anymore. It was simply baggage. I had my memories — that was enough. It was time to let go.

Shortly after that time, I was inspired by a speaker who demonstrated how he had carried everything he owned on his back for two years while serving in the army during World War II. I immediately thought about all the "things" I had accumulated over the years and decided to clean the rest of the house. First, I emptied my closets and filled four trash bags of clothes that I had held onto "just in case they might fit again." As I drove to the Salvation Army to drop off the bags, I realized that I had just released some of my own clutter that had been holding me back.

It's amazing how we hold onto all the junk from our pasts. As I continue my process of cleaning my house and office, I feel more and more a sense of closure on my past and a new freedom to move forward with my life. Some people may argue that clutter inspires creativity. Think about it this way — if all that clutter distracts you from accomplishing what you need (or want) to do, get rid of it. "Cleaning house" can be an overwhelming project. Start in one corner of one room and do a little bit each day. It's not going to happen overnight. Another option is to contact the National Association of Professional Organizers (512-454-8626). This organization can provide you with the name of a professional organizer who will come into your home and/or office and help you with this process.

At this point in my life, instead of cluttering my mind with "junk" from the past, I have committed to walking several miles a day to exercise my body, enjoy the outdoors, and free my mind for thinking creatively about new adventures.

Is your life cluttered with unimportant things or people who hold you back? How about your career?

Are you willing to let go of your clutter?

What steps can you take to free yourself for more stimulating endeavors?

Uninspiring Activities

I once asked my mother, "What am I good at?" "Chris, you sew beautifully," she responded. Yes, I was nimble with a needle. I had learned how to sew as a young teenager out of necessity. I desperately wanted a beautiful wardrobe to be just as stylish as my best friend, an only child who was doted on by her parents and grandmother. But nothing was ever handed to me. If I wanted to be in vogue, I had to work for it. I recall my mother giving me $3.50 for round trip bus fare, fabric, a pattern, and all the notions. Needless to say, I had to buy the cheapest material.

Sewing was a good experience that taught me resourcefulness and perseverance. As a young married woman with two small children and a limited budget, the sewing was useful. I made curtains, bedspreads, tablecloths, clothes for my kids, clothes for my husband, gifts for relatives, bathing suits, coats, hats, belts, and other accessories. I could sew anything well. However, there was one problem — I never enjoyed it.

Once I was able to convince myself that I didn't need to continue doing something I was "good at," it freed me to dabble in activities that were much more gratifying. I especially enjoyed taking art classes. Sitting at the kitchen table and sketching a still life is much more gratifying than struggling with a piece of fabric. I may never be a master, but it's relaxing, creative, and enjoyable. Besides, it's a wonderful break from the everyday stresses of a busy life.

As a workshop facilitator, I sometimes have my participants work with a technique that gives them a visual representation of their life's activities. Take a piece of paper, draw a circle (or something that represents you) in the middle, and then draw several lines coming out from the circle. At the end of each line write down everything you are involved in. Include hobbies, career, volunteer work, church activities, clubs and professional organizations, family, friends, and other things that consume your time. Have fun and be creative with this project —

use colored paper, draw pictures, cut pictures out of magazines, use colored markers, add stickers. This provides you with a picture of your life and all the people, activities, and things that make demands on you and your time.

After my parents died, I became involved in various volunteer activities to keep me busy. At first I felt stimulated, but eventually I became overwhelmed with so much involvement and questioned my true enjoyment. The dream helped me to realize that I didn't need to continue with the activities that weren't self-satisfying. By using my workshop technique, I discovered the activities that were meaningful and gradually eliminated the rest. At first it was difficult to let go, but my life is much more manageable these days, and I'm beginning to accomplish the things that are truly important to me.

Are you still participating in meaningless activities?

What outdated projects or activities can you give up to make room for something that truly defines your own creativity?

What are the new, more meaningful activities you will now have time to do?

Fear

Fear is probably everyone's greatest obstacle. In my dream, I was fearful as I stood on the sidelines looking up at myself sitting on the balloon. The part of me on the balloon felt the fear but also experienced the excitement of the ride. Life cannot be an adventure without taking risks. If fear is holding you back, read the excellent book, *Feel the Fear and Do It Anyway*, by Susan Jeffers. When I realized that self-doubt was excess baggage, I was able to face one of my greatest fears — public speaking.

For years I had pondered taking a public speaking class, but I was one of those people who probably feared it even more than death. It was the words of a college professor back in the 1980s that encouraged me to face this fear: "If you can speak in front of a group of people and present yourself well, that will get you a lot further than any M.B.A." At the time I had been thinking about getting a Masters Degree in Business Administration, but her powerful words inspired me to opt for the public speaking class.

The real turning point for me, however, began in 1993 when I braved a blustery February morning to attend a local Toastmasters meeting. Toastmasters International is a non-profit organization dedicated to help individuals develop communication and leadership skills in a friendly, non-threatening environment. Through skill-building, Toastmasters prepares you to meet the challenges of real life situations. Remember: I was the quiet kid who went to my room and closed the door. Thanks to the skills and confidence I have developed as a Toastmaster over the past six years, I no longer close doors. I was able to turn my greatest fear into a speaking career that has taken me on an incredible ride.

Is fear holding you back from moving forward with your career or having exciting adventures in your life?

Are you ready to pilot an airplane, dive into the depths of the sea, join a Toastmasters club, or take that next step to enhance your career?

What steps will you take to overcome any fears that are holding you back from accomplishing what you want in life?

So far, I have enjoyed my adventures on the hot air balloon. That's only because my childhood roots no longer hold me back from accomplishing exciting things in my life. Are you ready to let go of your excess baggage to start each day with a creative beginning? Where will your adventures take you and what will you accomplish along the way? Set goals for yourself, but know that the balloon may take you to places you never imagined. That's part of the intrigue. Be sure to search for messages along the way. For example, shortly after I received Ethel

Cook's yellow sticker, I read my horoscope in a magazine that said, "Just do it."

Life is a series of choices. You can choose to hold onto the baggage, or you can choose to soar.

ABOUT
CHRISTINA BERGENHOLTZ, M.ED.

C hristina Bergenholtz, M.Ed, is a consultant, educator and speaker. She helps individuals in corporations, associations and educational organizations develop winning skills in writing, speaking, mind mapping, creative thinking and creating new beginnings for themselves. Participants in her programs discover new ideas, develop practical techniques, break barriers to personal and professional success and have fun in the process! Christina holds memberships in various professional organizations, including the National Speakers Association, and is an adjunct faculty member of Quinsigamond Community College where she teaches verbal communication skills.

Contact Information:
Christina Bergenholtz
P.O.Box 301
Grafton, MA 01519
phone: (508) 839-5139
fax: (508) 887-9556
e-mail: chrismhb@aol.com

How to Turn Dreams and Goals into Achievements

by Bruce S. Wilkinson, CSP

Believe it or not, many of the most successful men and women in the world did not have everything handed to them on a silver platter and did not succeed in either business, sports, or their personal lives without having failed many times. In fact, many of them have felt discouraged, dejected, lost, lonely, worthless, and that they would never accomplish anything in their lives. Sound familiar? But most of the successful people I've admired over the years have had several other things in common. They all had goals and dreams, and they achieved them through hard work, overcoming hardships, perseverance, and with the help of others.

Successful and happy people are also big dreamers, and they know early on that no dream is too big and that very few of their dreams will come true without establishing a series of goals and strategies that will enable them to achieve their dreams.

Athletes are Big Dreamers

Some of these same successful dreamers are great athletes who are widely recognized as leaders by example. By receiving so much media exposure, they give the rest of us glimpses of the joy of success. As a result, people young and old tend to want to know how they achieved their dreams and goals and how they could be more like the successful athletes.

These disciplined and self-motivated athletes also have an effect on their less motivated teammates, which, in turn, helps them in achieving their dreams as well. You see, it's true. Enthusiasm is contagious! I think that Dick Enberg, nine-time Emmy Award-winning broadcaster, described these types of leaders best when he said, "The saddest thing that can happen in a life, I feel, is to under-dream." Most of the Hall of Famers, he said, had big dreams, and they knew how to clear life's hurdles in order to win! Track star and now transplant surgeon, Carlton Young, put it another way: "Shoot for the stars. You may not get the stars, but you may get the moon."

Achievement Tip #1 — Turning Dreams Into Goals

Find time in your busy schedule once a week to dream a little, and write that time down in your personal or business calendar so you won't forget. Once you start dreaming, set up a list of goals along with strategies, tactics, and action items to reach each goal. Don't forget to dream BIG. Just think. What would your goals be if you knew that you couldn't fail? These are the goals that I would pursue.

The following questions may give you some highway assistance while traveling along the road to your dreams:

A. Do you take the time to visualize your dreams and your success?

☐ Yes   ☐ No

TIP: Take a couple of minutes each day to picture yourself as the person you want to be and where you want to be. Now picture yourself confident, prepared, well-disciplined, and in control of the obstacles that you will face to succeed. Keep detailed notes on how you will overcome these obstacles by writing them in a Dream Book or journal.

B. Are you creating strategies, tactics, and action items to reach your goals?

☐ Yes   ☐ No

TIP: Put a divider in your Dream Book (or three-ring binder) for each goal you will need to fulfill your dream, and develop an action plan with time lines and dates to have them completed. Get a teammate or close friend to help hold you accountable for your commitments. Carlton Young, M.D. says that he approaches the operating room to do an organ transplant precisely the same way he used to step up to the blocks to run track: "Okay, I've got to get from point A to point B and I've got to do it right."

C. Do you have a way to remind yourself of what your goals are each day?

☐ Yes　　☐ No

TIP: This can be done by notes that can be seen daily, by starting each day glancing at your Dream Book, by using a computer software program, or by keeping a pocket-size list of goals by the phone to read while you are on hold on the telephone.

D. Do you tackle the list of hard and unpleasant tasks first? What about the most important task?

☐ Yes　　☐ No

TIP: Prioritize your list of tasks, and then tackle the hard ones first. Make a checklist to mark them off to give you a sense of accomplishment. Don't save all of the hard tasks for last, or you will be in a constant state of stress both at work and at home. *Don't forget to focus.* Former professional football player and retired NFL coach Raymond Berry said, "You don't aim at the bull's eye. You aim at the center of the bull's eye!"

Overcoming Hardships and Failures to Reach Success

When I was a teenager, I had typical short-term goals. They were called the weekend. I also had long-term goals. They were called next weekend! These types of fun goals, as I called them, ended when my father died of a heart attack when I was 16. At first, I thought that I would never be able to overcome his death, and I had to go to work to support myself and help my mother. I even wondered if I would be a failure or even be able to go to college. But my mother and father had given me the character to overcome hardships and failures, as well as knowledge of how to learn from them to be successful. Besides, some things are just out of your control. John Wooden, retired NCAA championship basketball coach, states, "Don't let what you cannot do interfere with what you can do." He was right!

One hardship that Americans do not have to overcome is the privilege of their birthplace. Americans should always be thankful that we were born in a country where our goals and dreams are easier to reach just because of the great country that we live in. I am almost always more impressed with those successful men and women who started in life with much less than what we started with in the United States.

Take New York Yankee pitcher Mariano Rivera, who, as a closer (relief pitcher), helped his team win three World Series out of four, making the Yankees the team of the '90s. Mariano had not given up a run in post-season games since 1997 and had not given up a run for three months of games going into the 1999 World Series against the Atlanta Braves. In fact, Mariano Rivera was named the 1999 World Series Most Valuable Player (MVP) for his effort in striking out so many Atlanta Brave batters in his two World Series-saving games as a closer. Being awarded the MVP is an incredible accomplishment for a part-time relief player.

That's not bad for a 6'2", 170 lb., 29-year-old from Panama who grew up spending days at a time in a small fishing boat to help his Dad look for sardines to make fish flour. In helping to help take care of his sister and two brothers, Mariano would make a baseball glove out of a piece of cardboard. He would then cut holes in the cardboard for his fingers using the cardboard to protect the palm of his hand. Mariano, during breaks in the World Series, showed some of the media how he made this cardboard glove. To this day, he sometimes makes one and puts it in this back pocket to remind him where he came from.

Mariano Rivera's coaches say that his confidence is always high and his will to succeed at all costs is always strong. In fact, his success means so much to his countrymen that the country of Panama nearly shuts down to watch him on television when he pitches.

Achievement Tip #2 — Overcoming Hardships and Disappointments

Everyone has hardships and disappointments to overcome, especially athletes. As Lee Roy Selmon, pro football player and now associate athletic director, University of South Florida, states, "One of the most important things I've learned from sports is that you just don't win every game. And you're not supposed to. It sounds mundane, but life is like that. You're not supposed to win every game."

Ask yourself the following questions in determining how to overcome hardships and disappointments.

A. Am I confident in my abilities, and can I learn from my mistakes?

☐ Yes   ☐ No

B. Do I have the strength to overcome the loss of money, a job, or the death of a loved one or close friend?

☐ Yes   ☐ No

C. Was what happened to me out of my control and unavoidable?

☐ Yes   ☐ No

D. Could I have prepared or studied more?

☐ Yes   ☐ No

E. Can I prepare differently in the future and avoid making the same mistakes?

☐ Yes   ☐ No

Take a lesson from a hard-working athlete who knew how to come from behind, John Wilson, college football player and retired president of Washington and Lee University: "In college, I was on a team that lost only one game in three years. But you know what? In almost every single one of those games, we were behind at half time. Think about it."

Turning Perseverance into Achievement

It sounds easy, doesn't it? Just dream big, come up with some defined goals, put your hardships and mistakes behind you, and you can win the gold! Well, that's at least part of the winning formula. Another key characteristic that most winning athletes have is perseverance.

According to Merlin Olsen, college and professional football great and now a professional actor and spokesperson, "Perseverance isn't just the willingness to work hard. It's that, plus the willingness to be stubborn about your own belief in yourself."

When I think of perseverance, one name stands out among all the rest — Lance Armstrong. On October 8, 1996, a somber doctor told Lance, a former world champion cyclist, that he was probably not going to be able to compete for a while, if ever. Lance had a lethal form of testicular cancer with a 20% to 50% survival rate. The next day, he had surgery to remove the malignant testicle. He then found out that the cancer had spread to his lungs and abdomen. Lance began a 12-week course of chemotherapy five days later. The doctors told him that they had found 8-10 golf ball-sized lumps of cancer in his lungs. After two weeks of chemo, they found the cancer had migrated to his brain. He underwent six hours of surgery. He then had drugs pumped into him for four hours a day, and he was hooked to IV bags for the other 20 hours to counteract the toxic side effects. Twelve months later, Lance was training 30-50 miles a day on his bike. Thirty-three months after the cancer was discovered, Lance Armstrong became the first American, on an American team, on an American bike, to win the Tour de France with an average speed of 24.9 miles per hour, through 2,306 miles of both flat and mountainous terrain — the fastest rate in 86 years of the race. All this after the French racing team had broken his contract and dropped him after they had publicly supported him when he found out about the cancer.

At the finish line in Paris, Lance said, "That cancer is smart. It's aggressive like me. It has tactics that can change and ways it can resist. I just said what I've always said about racing — whatever it takes to win!" Lance closed his press conference with the following statement: "If you ever get a second chance in life — go all the way!"

You see, perseverance is about trying and giving it your very best. Quoting once again from Lee Roy Selmon, pro football player and now Associate Athletic Director for the University of South Florida: "I don't have a philosophy of winning — I have a philosophy of trying. If you put forth an effort that encompasses your very best — all your intensity, all your enthusiasm — then you can stop worrying about the outcome, because you've done all you can do. By that definition, you're already a winner."

Achievement Tip #3 — Turning Perseverance into Achievement

There are no tips to learn perseverance. Just get over it, don't ever quit, and get it done! Just kidding. Of course, there are tips. Sometimes, perseverance just comes from within. Sometimes it comes from how you were brought up or whether or not you have a competitive nature. Here are some questions to ask yourself before tackling a huge task or trying to accomplish something that very few people have done or can do:

A. Do I set a goal and quit or lower the goal if the task becomes too hard?

☐ Yes   ☐ No

B. When things get tough, do I work even harder when it comes to succeeding?

☐ Yes   ☐ No

C. Do I keep my goals a secret in case I fail or decide to quit?

☐ Yes   ☐ No

These are great questions to ask yourself on a routine basis. You may even wish to ask the opinions of others who know you well and don't mind being honest with you. But in the end, it's as simple as this: You don't get everything that you want or deserve in life. However, you can get most of the things that you work hard for and earn.

Achieving Dreams and Goals Through the Help of Others

One of the best ways to achieve all of your dreams and goals is to ask for help from others. There are usually lots of people who are willing to help others, but sometimes we are too proud to ask. Yet, many of the successful athletes and sports celebrities today would not be successful had they not decided to work as part of a team. Like the military, each team member must be motivated and disciplined not only to perform their duties, but to have the confidence that their teammates will do the same. These team members must also be prepared to step up and pick up the slack or make a big play when their teammates can't.

The best example I can think of to demonstrate this would be the dramatic come-from-behind victory by the United States Ryder Cup team. It was the closing match between the United States and Team Europe. The U.S. team finished Saturday's round down 10 to 6, and there had never been a team in Ryder Cup history that had come back from that type of deficit on the last day. On Saturday night, Team Captain Ben Crenshaw told both his team and the media that they needed to keep the faith. He said that there was so much passion on this team and asked everyone to do his job and to never stop believing. "I'm a big believer in fate," he said, "and I have a great feeling about tomorrow's final match." He kept reminding his team about the history of The Country Club in Brookline, Massachusetts, the scene of the 1913 U.S. Open Championship where a 20-year-old American caddy by the name of Francis Ouimet made two 20' putts in the final round and the playoff on the 17th green to beat English heroes Ted Ray and Harry Vardon.

On Sunday morning in the final match, the Americans won eight single matches and halved one to upset the European team in a 14 to 13 victory. And it was on the 17th green that Justin Leonard sunk a 50' putt to win it for the Americans. Oh, and by the way, Francis Ouimet's old house still sits across the street, from that same 17th green.

Was the U.S. team's victory due to fate, faith, hard work, perseverance, dreaming, goal setting, or getting a little help from others? I think that it was a little bit of everything.

Achievement Tip #4 — Achieving Goals Through the Help of Others

There will always be men and women who will become successful without the help of others, or do they just think that they have done it on their own? Ask yourself the following questions to determine the roles others have played in your success to date:

A. Name some of the teachers who had an impact on either your personal or business success. Who taught you integrity, character and right from wrong?

B. Name at least three athletes whom you have always admired and mentioned to your children as positive role models.

C. Name a mentor whom you both respect and admire.

D. Name a historical/political figure or fictional character who inspires you and explain why.

E. Name someone you admire or who you want to be more like who has made sacrifices for a cause or to reach a goal.

F. Who in your life motivates you to be the best that you can be?

G. Finally, name a family member or loved one who will never give up on you even when you want to give up on yourself.

Keep in mind that you don't actually have to know people for them to be role models. Some of them may just be great men or women that you've read about. But you will never forget the role models that you've known in person or with whom you have had the privilege of playing together as teammates in organized sports or as comrades in the military where you had to watch each other's back. The hard part in receiving hands-on help from people that you respect is the act of asking for help itself since some successful people do not want others to think that they need any assistance of any kind. Don't let this attitude stop you from asking for help. Most dreamers and successful people do. Even athletes! Just remember to return the favor when asked and agree to be a mentor to someone else who also has a big dream or a goal to achieve. Being asked to mentor another person is the highest form of flattery, and you will be surprised about all of the great information that you will remember when you are helping someone else. Now you can use this great knowledge to make some new dreams all over again.

My final example on achieving goals comes from a movie entitled *"A League of Their Own,"* the true story of the women who played organized baseball for a living (and to entertain others) while most of the men were off fighting in World War II. Tom Hanks plays the over-the-hill baseball player who manages the team, and he's talking to Geena Davis, who is about to quit right before the championship series because her wounded husband has returned from the war. Geena says, "I quit. Baseball is just too hard!" Tom Hanks replies, "It's supposed to be hard. If it wasn't hard, everyone could do it. That's what makes it great!"

As you can see, the art of turning dreams and goals into achievements must be considered as a life-long process or journey that never really ends. So always aim high, shoot for the stars, and set tough goals for yourself on a routine basis. It will be hard and there will be sacrifices along the way, but, remember, you are reaching for great dreams!

ABOUT
BRUCE S. WILKINSON, CSP

*B*ruce *S. Wilkinson, CSP, is a management consultant, motivational keynote speaker, workplace trainer, and implementation specialist, who reinforces personalized messages with both humor and enthusiasm. He has degrees in both Safety Engineering and Occupational Safety and Health. Bruce is a member of the Board of Directors of the National Speakers Association and is one of fewer than 400 people worldwide to earn the prestigious Certified Speaking Professional (CSP). Besides his personalized keynote programs, he has developed and presented programs on effective leadership, communication, change, self-motivation, managing and motivating employee behavior, humor at work, customer service, disciplining with dignity, substance abuse, safety and health, violence in the workplace and sexual harassment.*

As president of Workplace Consultants, Inc., a nationally recognized speaking, training and consulting firm, he has presented in 49 states delivering enthusiastic messages to clients such as AT&T, Hershey's Chocolates, local governments, Lucent Technologies, Sara Lee, Six Flags Theme Parks, U.S. Air Force, various school boards, and Xerox.

Contact Information:
Bruce Wilkinson
Workplace Consultants, Inc.
1799 Stumpf Blvd., Bldg. 3, Suite 6B
Gretna, LA 70056
phone: (504) 368-2994
fax: (504) 368-0993
e-mail: SpeakPoint@aol.com

MULTITASKING: GETTING THINGS DONE RIGHT, ON TIME AND UNDER BUDGET

by Jan Cannon, M.B.A., Ph.D.

Have you ever had the feeling that there was too much to do and not enough time to get it all done? Have you tried to organize your time each morning only to find by the middle of the day that you'd gotten nothing done that you wanted to? Or maybe you have lots of great ideas bouncing around in your head, but you never seem to make any progress getting them to become reality.

If any of these describe you, you have a lot of company. Today's fast-paced world almost demands that we all do more. We have cell phones to be available any time and any place. Fax machines ring any hour, day or night, with preprogrammed dialing. E-mail makes us instantly connected with anyone around the world with the expectation that we will respond to any messages within a day — at the most. Access to information on our computers makes reports and analysis something to be developed in hours or days, not weeks, months, or even quarters as in the past.

This chapter offers a few helpful hints on how to cope with all that is demanded of you working in today's business world, whether as an employee or an entrepreneur, compiled from the many books I've read, audiotapes I've listened to in my car, and clients I've worked with over the years as a small business consultant. One task that rarely gets done is all the reading you want to do. I offer you this section as my *Cliff's Notes* version of many of the books you might have on your list — or bookshelf.

Success at work is a lot like driving a car: you know where you're going, but you have to deal with the traffic along the way.

All the experts agree on one thing: keep the "big picture" in mind when you are involved in your daily tasks. It's a little like looking at the forest once in a while instead of just the trees. With a clear picture of where you're headed, it's easier to make decisions along the way that will help you get there. As the Cheshire cat in Alice's wonderland advised — if you don't know where you're going, any path will take you there. So, to begin, make some goals: short-term for the next 6 months, long-range for the next 3-5 years, and mid-range for in between.

Goals should be specific, in writing, and reviewed often. Once you have goals you can decide what you need to do to reach them, breaking them down into small chunks that then become part of your action plan. A plan that sits in a drawer is not very useful — so plan your work and then *work your plan.*

Create a system that you can use to keep you aware of your long-term goals as you plan each day.

Skipper Hull, owner of Little Foreign Car Garage, made a visual plan that helps him stay focused on his day-to-day tasks, and at the same time, work toward his long-term goals. He bought a cork bulletin board, about 36" x 48," that he attached to the wall above his desk in the shop office. On different colored PostIt™ notes he lists all the tasks he's thought of that need to be done to reach his goals of 1) buying his building, 2) opening a second auto repair and racing shop, 3) expanding his used car sales, 4) painting and reroofing his house, and 5) playing basketball twice a week. (Note that business and personal goals are both on his chart.) Each goal is assigned a different color PostIt note, and slips are added as he thinks of new things that need to get done — and subtracted as they are finished. He has a very colorful visual reminder of what's important to him — and what he has to do. By writing down the smaller tasks he can make progress toward each goal without feeling overwhelmed by the whole project. With the bulletin board on the wall beside his desk, he can look at it every day to decide the steps he'll take next.

He installed a similar chart in the shop for the mechanics to use for their repair work. When cars come in for repair, they are "triaged" by amount of time required and difficulty to repair to better schedule the day's work (much like hospital emergency room nurses who decide which injuries or health problems need immediate attention and which can wait). Once each car is assessed for the amount and type of work that needs to be done, a slip is made out that goes on the board, noting how long the repair is expected to take and any parts or special tools that need to be ordered. The work slips are arranged by technician so that the workload can be balanced, a decision that had unexpected effects in boosting morale among the mechanics since they now could see that none of them was being asked to do more than the others. Weekly revenue goals were posted and measured against the daily repair orders, again creating incentives for the mechanics to be more productive so they could reach the expected revenues that determined their profit-sharing.

Clearly, for Little Foreign Car Garage, having long-term goals and daily tasks visible to everyone in the shop has worked for both increasing productivity and personal satisfaction. And most of the goals are being met. Think about a system that will work for you and try it for a month.

To set goals, start with ideas.

Ideas can come from many places. Start with reflections on challenges facing you in your work or your life. Ask questions. Pose problems. Create alternative answers, and then evaluate the consequences of those alternatives. Think about changes you would like to see: in your job, in your community, in your relationships. What would you like to learn more about? How can you improve something?

Once you've decided on your goals, the action steps will come next. They need to be broken down into the smallest possible parts. It's always easier to do a piece of the whole than to try to attack it all at once. Like eating an elephant, it's one bite at a time. Little pieces can be done regularly, or at least frequently, and eventually the whole project will be finished. Reflect on what you've done. Evaluate your methods and results and take new action, if need be. Then on to another idea, another goal.

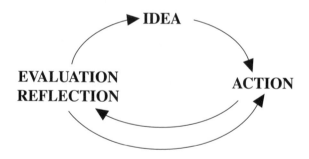

**Getting control of your time and your paperwork
can be the biggest challenge.**

Are you ever interrupted when you're working on something, and then never quite get back to the task? Do you go to meetings and ask yourself why you are there? Is your "inbox" overflowing? Are your office plants dead because you can't find time to water them? Do you exercise every day? Managing your interruptions, phone calls, mail, meetings, etc. can become easier if you follow these 10 steps.

1. Have daily, weekly, monthly, and yearly goals. With clear goals you will be able to decide which activities are the most important, which can be safely postponed, which you can ignore completely. Learn to say "no."

2. Set priorities — don't accept deadlines you can't meet. Be honest with yourself and others when promising to get work done. Don't force yourself to compromise your quality, your personal time, or your other commitments to meet an unrealistic deadline.

3. Schedule your days so that you have quiet work hours and specific times when you're available to others. Know when you do your best work in the day and then keep that time for your highest-priority activities. Take telephone messages that you return on your personal "off-peak" time rather than answering the phone each time it rings. Don't let people interrupt you; set up appointments or have "open door" time scheduled for drop-ins. Define what you will do — and when.

4. Never handle paper more than twice — once is better. Assign mail to A, B, and C priority piles, and throw away the C pile without opening it. Either act on something you read, pass it on, or throw it out. Don't file it with the expectation that "some day" you'll get to read it. This is one area where you should show no mercy.

5. Skim read. There is so much information that we want to know but so little time to absorb it. Learn how to skim newspapers and magazines for key ideas. Look at tables of contents or indexes and read only those parts you find important. Delete e-mail you suspect is "junk mail" without opening it. Information overload is all around us.

6. Use technology. Computers, planners, conference calls, the Internet all can be used efficiently and effectively to maximize your time and attention on your priority tasks. Learn how to use them effortlessly.

7. Attend only the most important meetings. Is there a detailed agenda? Do you have to attend, or can others represent your ideas? Can

it be held via telephone? Always take something else to work on. Meetings are a huge time (and money) waster.

8. Delegate. This might seem impossible, especially if you work alone, but it can be done by hiring people part-time to do those tasks you never seem to get done. Learn to give good directions so that you can be confident that the finished product will be what you expected.

9. Do business during coffee breaks and lunch. Developing relationships with others is the key to success in this fast-changing business environment. Why not take the opportunity to get to know colleagues, suppliers, even competitors better in a social setting?

10. Exercise at least 20 minutes every day. Even if it means walking around the hallways or up and down the stairs in your building, get yourself moving to clear your head and boost your energy. Your brain will function better with some new blood (and you might even lose a few pounds).

Be realistic about what you can accomplish in a day.

If you set 3-4 priority activities per day and get them done, give yourself a pat on the back. Priority activities are those which move you toward your goals, not crises that need to be dealt with immediately that may have no long term positive consequences. One challenge is to be realistic about how long tasks take. Give each task your best "guesstimate"about how much time must be invested to get it done — and then add 1/3 more.

Just like you schedule appointments with others, schedule appointments with yourself, using a calendar system that works for you. I plan my Friday afternoons from 3:00-5:00 to clean up my desk and office. This is my time to read articles I've set aside all week, file those client records that got piled on the top of the file cabinet rather than in it, prepare the additions to my database that get sent to my "virtual" assistant for inputting — basically tidy-up the office so that I can leave it knowing I'll be ready for action on Monday morning.

Your calendar should be your favorite tool for planning and recording your goals. Schedule time to work on those activities that will move you toward them. Make activities related to your goals as important in your week as any meeting you may have with clients, bosses, referrals, etc.

Schedule "emergency" time each week.

Pat Brennan, owner of Hair Pluss, an eight-person hair and nail salon, specializes in hair color correction. Hair color correction is needed when hair highlighting or dyeing doesn't come out as expected and some adjustments need to be made. It's unlikely that a client will have the stylist who caused the problem try to fix it. Instead, she'll find someone else. Enter Pat. She loves to figure out what went wrong and then make the client happy by redyeing the hair. What this requires in her schedule, however, is "emergency" time. Like a dentist who has to leave room in the schedule for the unexpected toothache, Pat leaves a two-hour block of time every Thursday afternoon for anyone with a color correction problem. This way she can make a potential new client happy and not make herself crazy trying to squeeze someone else into her already full schedule. If there's no color correction scheduled, Pat takes an hour to go to the nearby gym and treat herself to a short workout and a sauna. I think some weeks she hopes there won't be anyone in the "emergency" time slot.

Having an "emergency" time set aside each week would work for anyone. Maybe you need it more often, but leaving a little wiggle room in your weekly schedule goes a long way toward keeping stress levels manageable. You, too, could take a well-deserved break if nothing filled that time.

Get those ideas and plans on paper so you don't have to keep remembering them.

Do you ever wake up in the middle of the night with a great solution to a problem and then forget it by morning? Do you sometimes think of things you need to buy at the office supply store, but when you're roaming the aisles can't remember what they all were? Writing down your good ideas or other things you want to remember opens up brain space for new thoughts. I know I can use all the brain space I have some days.

It's possible you have little scraps of paper with all your ideas on them floating around your office, in your jacket pockets, in your purse. Or maybe you're a great list maker. I'd like to suggest something to do with all those great ideas, no matter how you collect them.

Once a week have a priority planning session. Nancy Hammett, a senior economics researcher at Abt Associates, meets me every Sunday morning at 7:00 for coffee. We both bring our planners and our stacks of ideas, conference notices, and lists of things we thought of during the week. For an hour we fill in our calendars for the week, scheduling time to think, plan and write as well as meet others. I start with a blank sheet of paper and list the major tasks for the week ahead. I also list those long-term projects that I don't want to forget, although I may not get started on them immediately. Only when I have my new list do I look over the list from the week before. Are there activities that I still want to do from that list? What are the next steps to get them done? Nancy makes her own lists, on several pieces of paper, one for each ongoing project she oversees. The important thing is to know during the week that when ideas come up, they don't need to be thought about or acted on immediately because Sunday morning there will be time to do that.

There's no one best method for this kind of planning. What's important is that we both do our weekly planning. By meeting each other, we have built in some accountability (and maybe a little guilt if one of us doesn't show up). Surprisingly, we don't talk too much, but do focus on making our schedules. And those schedules include more than work activities.

Life needs to be balanced. Those hours spent in parenting or civic activities are just as important as those spent developing a new marketing campaign or paying the bills — so put them on your calendar. The planning often determines the quality of your activities for the week. Lots more can get done with a list, a schedule, and a plan. Think about how you behave the few days before you go on vacation. Things get done in a burst of energy. You tick off the items on your list in anticipation of a time away from your work. What would you accomplish if you worked at that level every day? Could you? Try it for a week and see.

You now have some new tools to help you get things done right, on time, and under budget. Setting goals, prioritizing your activities, and guarding your time all help lead to success. If you keep asking yourself, "Is this the most important thing I can be doing right now?," you'll find your goals and priorities will guide you. You will become the model of an effective and productive member of your organization and your reward will be, at the very least, your own sense of accomplishment and to have reached your goals. Enjoy the journey.

My teachers:

Tom Hopkins, *Mastering the Art of Selling*
Tom Winninger, *Personal Performance*
Stephen Covey, *First Things First*
Anthony Robbins, *Awaken the Giant Within*
Spencer Johnson, *"Yes" or "No"*
Terri Lonier, *Working Solo*
Hal Wright, *How to Make 1000 Mistakes in Business
    and Still Succeed*
Alyce Cornyn-Selby, *The Procrastinator's Success Kit*
Peter Senge, *The Learning Organization*
Alan Lakein, *How to Get Control of Your Time and Your Life*
Barbara Sher, *Wishcraft*
Rebecca Maddox, *Inc. Yourself*
Alan Weiss, *Million Dollar Consulting*

ABOUT
JAN CANNON, M.B.A., PH.D.

*J*an Cannon, Ph.D., is a business coach and strategic planner who works
*with business owners, entrepreneurs, consultants and professionals to
improve their businesses and their quality of life. She helps develop marketing solutions, sales demonstrations, budgets and new focus or expansion
plans. And she helps clients "get a life" in the process. Her 15 years of
business experience includes manufacturing children's clothes, owning and
operating a career advisement center, teaching at Northwestern University,
and hosting the weekly television show, "It's All about Work". Jan is one of
the on-line specialists at CIO.com's Ask the Experts.*

Contact Information:
Jan Cannon
Cannon Business Development
38 Orchard Street
Belmont. MA 02478-3010
phone: (617) 484-5998 or (800) 550-4544
e-mail: Coach@Cannon4Success.com
web: www.Cannon4Success.com

INGREDIENTS FOR SUCCESS:
HUMOR, LAUGHTER AND PLAY

by Marianne Frederick, MHSA

Not long ago, I was seated in a remote section of the waiting area at the Seattle airport, with yellow legal-pad sheets spread over the adjacent seats, busily working on this chapter. I glanced up and my eyes wandered to a man walking toward me, a broad grin on his face. My initial reaction was that I was about to be accosted by some lonely soul meandering around the airport. (These people seem to find me the way a St. Bernard finds injured skiers.) I was quickly relieved to see, by his collar, that he was a minister. It's always nice to have a preacher on your flight. It's better than flight insurance. It seems the button I was wearing was like a beacon to him. It is bright yellow with hot pink lettering that reads, "Enjoy Life: This is Not a Dress Rehearsal." Now this is no ordinary-sized button. I remember the words of a young woman who saw me coming up an escalator once, "Look at that woman . . . that button is as big as her head," she remarked to her colleague. The minister was intrigued and I explained that the button frequently creates smiles and I told him how humor helps me to accomplish my goals.

I had just finished presenting two days of harassment training and discovered that utilizing a sense of humor in teaching the classes had been the most important ingredient in making the attendees more comfortable with such a controversial topic, and more willing to participate in the discussions. It was another example of the benefits that humor provides to me as an educator and a speaker. Can you benefit from utilizing a humorous perspective to accomplish your goals? As I see it, three ingredients to success in any growth-oriented business are *humor, laughter,* and *play*, and my goal here is to give you *five tips to heighten your humorous perspective.*

Humor and a sense of levity have been my staples as a physical therapist in a career that has spanned a score of years. (A score sounds shorter than twenty.) I have successfully used humor to enhance communication and learning, to decrease stress, to overcome barriers, and to create more energy. By focusing on positive emotions and those three ingredients, I am healthier, more quick-witted and better looking than ever. (No wrinkles, only laugh lines.) I believe that we can increase the intellectual assets of our organizations by encouraging our associates to learn to take the spirit of play into the workplace. Humor, however, is like a condiment, which, if used indiscriminately or when you don't know the other ingredients (i.e. people) very well, may create a disaster. Mark (my favorite husband) told me I am extremely presumptuous in using cooking terms, saying that I have not spent enough time in the kitchen to learn them. He is quick to tell people that if it weren't for the microwave, he would starve to death. This is also the same man who brags to his friends that he has found the perfect place to hide my Christmas presents. He just puts them in the oven. I really am a good cook, only sometimes I need to look up the location of the kitchen in the house plans.

Humor

One of my favorite comedians, Bill Cosby, believes, "If you can find humor in anything, you can survive it." You don't have to be a comedian or even remember a joke to show that you have a sense of humor. I like to remind people that humor is an attitude . . . so is love . . . so is faith, and with each, we can find more effective ways to approach life's daily aggravations, irritations, and frustrations. Demonstrating that you have a sense of humor can be as simple as smiling at someone's attempts at humor or responding with a laugh even after you have heard someone's favorite story over and over for years. An attitude of joy, enthusiasm, and other positive emotions are energy replacers while stress, anger, hostility and negative attitudes are energy drainers. Humor is a re-energizer . . . it's the power behind that long-eared bunny as he makes his way around the country banging his drum. Now some of us who are older, wiser, and maybe a little more deaf, aren't afraid to bang our drums loudly; it's a matter of finding your own beat. This beat can create a lightness in our step, a twinkle in our eye, and a grin that makes others wonder just what we've been up to.

Humor is often created because someone looks at life from a different perspective. A number of years ago my sister-in-law, Karen, and my nephew, Adam (who was 4 at the time), were standing in the front yard looking out over their neighborhood. Adam excitedly asked, "Mom, where are Kimberly and Angela going to live?" He was pleased that his two older cousins would be moving into the neighborhood soon and would be living close enough for them to play together daily. When Karen pointed to a brown house just two doors down, she knew he would be happy. She looked over at him only to see his little face, which had been filled with excitement and enthusiasm, turn pensive and his wide grin become a disappointed scowl as he replied, "But, that's so far away!" She was more than a little surprised by his remark until he finished his very perceptive analysis of the situation by continuing, ". . . you said I'm not allowed to cross the street by myself."

Laughter

If humor is the attitude, then laughter is humor transformed into a physical reality. I teach people about "Laughtercise," which is a set of silly gyrations which demonstrate the fact that even our address can make us laugh, if we approach it with the right attitude. John Kennedy once said, "There are three things which are real: God, human folly and laughter. The first two are beyond our comprehension. So we must do what we can with the third." When was the last time you laughed out loud? There are measurable benefits from hearty laughter as it impacts the circulatory, respiratory, endocrine, and immune systems. Years ago, the physical effects of laughter were described by Charles Darwin this way: "During excessive laughter, the whole body is often thrown backwards and shaken, or almost as often convulsed; respiration is much disturbed, the head and face become engorged with blood, the veins distend. Tears are freely shed." That doesn't quite instill in us the pleasant memories that we often have of times that we "laughed until we cried," but word choice can make a major difference between the scientist's and the humorist's view of the world. When we laugh until we cry, we create a positive benefit to the body, which, in part, is due to a tension release and also due to stress hormones being eliminated from the body. There is a chemical difference between tears of laughter and those we shed when we are peeling onions. I say, "Laughter, like peeling onions, will drive you to tears, but you won't end up with smelly fingers."

Laughter can be compared to exercise similar to stationary jogging and can significantly increase the heart rate, but there is the advantage of not having to squeeze into spandex outfits nor paying money to embarrass yourself in front of strangers at the YMCA. I was forced to go to the "Y," however, when, while practicing "step aerobics" upstairs at home one evening, I heard my husband's voice from the basement ask, "What are you doing up there . . . bowling?" At the "Y," I always chose to stand in the last row as far away from those mirrored walls as I could get. One evening when I first started working out, my heart was pounding so hard in my chest that I began to wonder if I was going to have a heart attack and drop dead in the middle of the "step aerobics" class. But then I remembered thinking it would be okay . . . "because I know CPR." Obviously, the blood was not making a full circuit through my brain when I had that little flash of insight.

Play

"People do not quit playing because they grow old. They grow old because they quit playing." Oliver Wendell Holmes thus explains an important correlation between play and the effects it has on physical, emotional, and mental development. Play is *fun*damental to life. Children who don't get the opportunity to play often have delayed brain development and physical skills. Play is not reserved for the young, though we can often learn important lessons from watching and listening to them. Their childlike innocence and open-mindedness allow them to see things in much different ways. Play in either physical or mental forms allows us to look at things from a unique perspective and can open our eyes and brains to other avenues by which we can solve daily dilemmas. When using the brain in creative and interactive ways, you keep it in better working condition. Remember the old adage: "If you don't use it, you lose it"?

Puzzles, brainteasers, and stimulating conversation are but a few of the ways to keep the mind active. I highly recommend the use of "brain tools," which I frequently find in toy stores and Big Lots, my favorite place to shop. When people say they are not creative, I encourage them to focus on thinking outside of their usual routine and to do things that are out of the ordinary for them. Play is not just for children, but it's easier to become playful around them. A couple of years ago, I answered my doorbell to two young boys about age nine. I was expecting the regular request to purchase wrapping paper or candy, so you can imagine my surprise and delight when (with all the seriousness that little boys can muster) they asked me in unison, "Do you need any detectives?" They went on to explain that they were good at solving mysteries and that if I needed a "detective," to please call them. I slipped back into the house for my calendar where I dutifully logged Joshua and Tyler's phone numbers under "D" in my telephone directory. No, I haven't had an occasion to call them, but every time I come across their names, I still smile as I remember their eager faces.

Five Tips to Heighten Your Humorous Perspective

1. Be a Kid Again and Dream BIG.

What is your BIG dream? How can you avoid losing sight of it? I remind myself to dream big with a black vinyl tote bag with the word BIG across it in large red letters. Visual reminders help me to stay focused on my goals. Taped to my bathroom mirror is a picture collage of those things that I want to achieve in my life. It even includes pictures of the British actor, Patrick Stewart (Captain Jean Luc Picard of the U.S.S. Enterprise), . . . be still my beating heart . . . but that is another dream. Humor is a way of keeping in touch with the kid inside of you, a way to regain some of the natural joy and enthusiasm of our youth. As I do programs for teenagers to help them prepare for college, I reinforce the issue that you can have a successful professional career *and* still enjoy the journey. My mission is to teach them that an appropriate sense of humor is as important a work skill as attitude, a proper work ethic, and having a professional mission.

Another visual reminder of my goals is a ceramic wind chime that is in the shape of a clown. It has a yellow bell-shaped bodice which carries the message, "Give me levity or give me death," while the legs in yellow-and-red striped stockings are the bell's clappers that dance in the wind.

2. Use Right Brain Playfulness to Enhance Creativity.

The right side of the brain is stimulated with humor, laughter, and a sense of playfulness. Joel Goodman, the founder of the Humor Project, Inc. in New York, describes humor and creativity as 'kissing cousins' and says, "if you want to develop your sense of humor, invite more creativity into your life — and vice versa."

A participant at one of my seminars demonstrated some creative thinking as she heard me complain about an obvious patch of gray hair on the crown of my head. She immediately suggested that it could easily be explained away by telling people that I must have just gotten my head too close to the ceiling while painting. I thanked her for a great line that I used until my next trip to the stylist to whom I gave search and destroy orders for the offending strands. Wilson has now started referring to those persistent gray hairs on the top of my head as "silver." Do you know that I have found that these "silver" ones don't bother me near as much as the "gray" ones did?

3. Find Some Favorite Props and/or a "Thinking Cap."

People often ask me where I get the props and hats that have become the cornerstones of my programs. I tell them, everywhere! Recently, a hat at the Kansas City airport caught my eye. It read, "Dear Dorothy, Hated OZ. Took the shoes. Find your own way home. (signed) Toto." I bought it. Does it make me laugh out loud? has now become part of my purchasing criteria.

I encourage you to be constantly on the lookout for things that make you laugh and smile. We must keep our eyes open and be ready for levity when it comes or be able to produce it when there is a need. Hats can help to achieve that end. You can use a hat as an attitude changer, a "thinking cap" to generate new ideas, or something just to keep people from bothering you when you are trying to get your work done without interruptions. (People who don't know you well are not likely to ask you about your hat . . . they will simply ask someone else about your sanity.) Last week I found a new prop which reminds me to laugh in the face of one of my least favorite chores. It's a large, red laundry bag which marks the amount of clothes inside and as the bag fills up, it reads from the bottom of the bag "Week 1". . . "Week 2" . . .

"Week 3" . . . "Naked." I can't help but laugh as I now find gathering the laundry a fun task rather than a chore.

We need to remember, the joy is in the journey. That morning my journey was to the post office. As I pulled out of the driveway in my Jeep, I noticed a young boy about eight years of age trudging slowly up the street toward the house. It was obvious that he carried a heavy load and his backpack wasn't the only thing slowing his steps as he walked reluctantly to school. I had packed my bags of hats into the back seat and then casually tossed my "ruby red lips" into the back end. I often used this pair of 24-inch-wide-ruby-red inflatable lips to illustrate enthusiasm, passion, and a love for what we do. As I drove around the corner and up the street, I noticed a whiff of exhaust fumes, but didn't realize that the rear door, which hadn't latched when I shut it, had quietly popped open. It was on my arrival at the post office, a half mile from home, that I was shocked to discover that the rear hatch was open and my lips were gone! I quickly took care of business and drove back home, retracing my route looking for my lips along the side of the road. It wasn't until I reached the driveway lipless, that I realized that the hatch must have opened when I first noticed those fumes . . . just around the corner from the house . . . exactly the route of that youngster on his way to school. Can you imagine the look of surprise that must have crossed his face as he came upon that 24-inch pair of lips in the middle of the street? I grin just thinking about it. Fortunately, I often buy duplicates of special props, so I did have a "spare set of lips" in the house. I enjoyed the humor of the situation, even more, when I realized that a higher power had decided that a little boy on his way to school needed my inflated ruby-red smile that day much more than I did.

4. Create a "Humor Reminder Binder" and/or a "Humor Journal."

A "Humor Reminder Binder" is a three-ring binder in which I ask you to place your precious collection of all those things that used to end up under magnets on your refrigerator door. Inside the binder are colorful pages in sheet protectors to hold every picture, card, or cartoon that strikes you funny and makes you smile or laugh out loud. It is a prescription for a healthier attitude, a respite from daily stresses, and a reward for hard work and/or play. You are encouraged to enjoy its contents daily and to add to it on a regular basis because it is good for your health.

A "Humor Journal" contains anything that happens to you, crosses your mind, or strikes you funny that you want to keep in writing for later use or a laugh. The journal is a record of those precious memories of a smile shared when you catch the eye of someone else who gets the joke that everyone else in the room missed. I'm a firm believer that we don't ever have to recreate the wheel when it comes to ideas, but often our best ideas, silly thoughts, or passing moments of wisdom will slip away unless we capture them in one place. I have also found that some of the funniest people are the writers of greeting cards, so that all I have to do is go searching for them. Another option is to buy a card that makes you laugh, address it, and ask the store manager to mail it to you in the next few weeks. When you receive it, you may have even forgotten that you had purchased it . . . so it will be another pleasant surprise to open it while you think to yourself, "Gee, that writing sure does look familiar."

5. Create A List of Accomplishments.

Have you created a list to help you keep track of the things that you want to accomplish each day? Add to the list as you complete other chapters:

☐ I helped to create smiles in people's lives, even across
   the telephone.

☐ I shared a sense of joy and wonder at being alive.

☐ I laughed out loud to the surprise and delight of other people.

☐ I carried a sense of playful and childlike anticipation into the day, looking for things that would make me smile and laugh, even at work.

☐ I kept a smile on my face through some tough times and found that I actually began to feel the way that I looked.

☐ (write in your own) . . .

☐ (here too) . . .

As you eagerly devour the rest of this book, you will get other ideas and perspectives on how to accomplish your goals in life. Humor, laughter, and play are but three of the ingredients offered as suggestions to help you to create energy, enthusiasm, and zest in your life. They will help to get your creative juices flowing with new ideas. Success in life is a matter of finding the right balance of ingredients and seasonings that will create a masterpiece. It's a necessary balance between the serious, accomplishment-oriented part of you and the creative, fun-loving part that generates the ideas from the right brain in the first place. Make the commitment to start new projects and accomplish new successes by flavoring your life and work with these special ingredients. If you need a visual reminder, just picture me with my red apron and chef's hat wearing a yellow button "as big as my head" that reads, "Enjoy Life: This is Not a Dress Rehearsal."

ABOUT
MARIANNE FREDERICK, MHSA

Marianne Frederick is a speaker, humorist and safety coach. Her expertise is in helping organizations create workplace environments that are healthy with co-workers who are more creative and productive. She sees her mission as providing groups with skills to humorously and creatively deal with changes and stressors in the workplace. Marianne has designed and taught "Mentor-based Safety Competency Skills" to help decrease the chance of injury while employees learn to perform the high-risk procedures that their jobs might entail. Marianne is a graduate of Ohio State University with a B.A. in physical therapy. She earned a master's degree in Health Services Administration (MHSA) from the Medical University of South Carolina, which she now claims refers to "Masters in Humorously Sharing Anecdotes!" Her client list includes Hoechst-Diafold, Clemson University, Fluor Daniel, and various business, education and government organizations.

Contact Information:
Marianne Frederick
WorkPlay, Inc.
14 Bridgewood Ave.
Taylors, SC 29687
phone: (864) 268-1541
fax: (864) 268-1541
e-mail: MFredck@aol.com

ATTITUDE + ACTION = ACCOMPLISHMENT

---

by Mary Kay Kurzweg

S heila* had one of the worst attitudes I had ever seen! During the Attitude Adjustment Seminar I was leading, she was indifferent, even distant — except during the times that she became hostile to others in the group, and once even to me. She didn't like her job, "hated" her ex-husband who was always late paying child support, and continually referred to her two kids as "the brat pack."

Well, I have to say, that was a long presentation. But not only did I make it through, somehow I connected with Sheila. By the end of the workshop she had become pleasant and was readily attacking the individual and group exercises I was suggesting to help a person build a more positive attitude.

I saw Sheila three months later at a follow-up session with her organization. I am always interested in seeing how people have adapted my information and ideas in real life and was excited to speak with Sheila. She entered the room smiling, looked me in the eye, and offered a pleasant and sincere, "Welcome back." She was quite nice during our conversation. She still had the same job within the organization, her ex-husband was still treating her poorly, and her children were "still a handful." In short, Sheila's circumstances had not really changed. Yet, clearly, she was different.

* Names have been changed to protect privacy.

When we talked, she shared that after the seminar her thoughts had turned to all the goals she had had before her marriage crumbled and her responsibilities escalated. The demands on her time as a single mother had put her desire for further education on hold. The financial situation was not good, and her social life was non-existent. Yet, wallowing in self-pity and hanging on to the anger were not making life better for her or her children.

I had urged the entire group to constantly look for opportunities to make their lives better — the opportunities are there! Sheila was listening. Sheila had begun taking an advanced computer course during her lunch hour, paid for by her employer. Her new skills would also mean new opportunities within the organization. She liked the friends she met at class, and her children enjoyed seeing her happy.

Her new, more positive attitude was wonderful, but it was only when it was combined with commitment to action that accomplishment could take place. This is true for all of us. It takes a good attitude combined with an action plan to accomplish your dreams.

A positive attitude is essential for anyone to enjoy and get the most out of life. But I've come to learn that a positive attitude isn't enough for those who want to attain all that they are capable of achieving. It is only when a positive attitude is combined with appropriate action that accomplishments can take place in a person's life. I have broken this down into a formula or a plan for success.

To accomplish what we want in life allows for personal happiness, satisfaction, and fulfillment. In short, accomplishments help each of us answer the question, "Why am I here?" or, as William Bridges described it in his book *Transitions*, "To act on the basis of what we really want is to say, 'I, a unique person, exist.' "

There are two key elements to combining attitude and action: deciding what you really want, and working to reach these goals and visions no matter what obstacles appear along the way.

Knowing What You Want

How true is the old saying, "If you don't know where you're going, any road will take you there." Too often people with real talents and capabilities seem to be drifting through life. They aren't focused; their lives are controlled by outside "things" (such as demanding family members or unsatisfying work), and, worst of all, they aren't excited about anything in their life!

A Compelling Future

To reach worthwhile accomplishments, a person must create what I call a compelling future. This "vision of the future" is the big picture of what it is a person wants to do, become, and have in life. A compelling future is, in other words, a person's deepest desires and wants.

Many of us are afraid to even consider what it is that we want. Our families, friends, and society in general often shape our attitudes about who we are and what we can become. I am certain that in the past you've heard or have even been given advice such as the following:

"A person can't make a decent living (being a musician, writing, gardening, etc.)."

"The only way to really get ahead is to (go to a four-year college, study computers, learn a foreign language, etc.)."

"Respectable people don't (quit their jobs and volunteer for the Peace Corps, put their family at risk by investing their savings on starting a new business, etc.)."

"You are too old to (go to college, start a new career, end a bad relationship, etc.)."

But "playing it safe" ultimately doesn't make it; it's unfulfilling, unexciting, and wears a person down mentally and physically. Despite the risks and fear of the unknown that's involved, one must set out to accomplish worthy things to make life truly meaningful and fun. M. Scott Peck says it best in his book *Further Along the Road Less Traveled:*

". . . to really seek the truth (in life), one cannot carve out a safe niche and hole up in it. One must blunder out there into the unknown, the mysterious."

To know what it is you want in life or to create compelling future goals, do the following:

• Go to a quiet place where you can be alone and uninterrupted for at least one hour.

• Using a notebook and pen, take three pieces of paper. Across the top of one, write "The Person I Want to Become"; across the second, write "The Things I Want to Accomplish in Life"; across the third, write "The People I Want in My Life."

• Sit quietly and reflect on each of these questions. Don't worry if "answers" don't immediately pop into your mind; simply give your inner being time to absorb, dream, and ponder.

• Begin writing everything that comes into your head. Don't hold back or censor your thoughts; let your ideas and imagination run wild!

• Review what you wrote. Now ask yourself this question: How close are these thoughts, dreams, and desires to what I am and have now?

Obligations, such as the need to make enough money to support yourself or support a family, weigh heavily on most people. But the courageous find a way to move in the direction of that compelling goal. Often when their dreams become realities, happiness, satisfaction and money soon follow. Consider these examples:

• Charmoon Richardson turned a twenty-year interest in mushrooms into a full-time business, "Wild About Mushrooms."

• Bill Gates dropped out of Harvard to start his own business . . . a little entity called "Microsoft" that has made Gates a billionaire several times over.

• Mary Kay Kurzweg (yes, that's me!) turned a love of speech and debate into a career as a professional speaker, trainer, and consultant.

A person doesn't have to start his or her own business to find fulfilling work. I know many people who are working for large organizations and enjoying all the stability of a steady salary, health insurance, and a retirement plan, yet are performing jobs they genuinely enjoy and want to pursue in life.

Ellen is one such example. I met Ellen in one of my job search seminars. This young woman, on government assistance at the time, landed a job as a nursing assistant in the dermatology department of a large hospital. Her supervisors and co-workers began to notice that Ellen was particularly effective explaining to people the various steps and products involved to treat each type of skin condition. She was promoted to skin care consultant, complete with commissions. Her sales were outstanding, and today she is financially independent, drives a new car, and just returned from a fabulous vacation!

Please note that I'm not suggesting that you run out and immediately begin following your dreams, particularly at the expense of those who depend upon you. Change requires time to implement, especially when it is a major life transition. What is critical, however, is that you know what it is that you want and never lose sight of the possibility of having it.

A leading photographer in our city who is responsible for many beautiful magazine covers spent almost 25 years in the electrical industry before being able to become a full-time professional photographer. Throughout those years, he studied and developed his talent. His business has been both successful and satisfying.

Goal Setting

Once you have the big picture, start developing goals to create that future. The goals are the specific outcomes that you want to accomplish within a set period of time. Goals are linked with our vision of the future the way bricks and lumber make up a house. Here's an example:

Compelling Future: I want to teach children.

Goal: Earn my teaching certificate within four years.

Goal: Send my resume to at least 25 schools within three months of obtaining my teaching certificate.

Goal: Secure a teaching position at an accredited school within nine months of obtaining my teaching certificate.

As you can see, effective goals always support the elements of a person's vision or plan for success. Other characteristics of effective goals include the following:

• They are specific. "Eat healthy food" is too vague. A better goal would be, "I will replace sweets with fresh fruit for one week beginning today."

• Goals are more effective when written down. Just thinking about what you want to do is a dream: we wish it would come true, but we don't want to work to make it happen. Written goals allow you to review your goals often, effectively helping "program" your subconscious mind.

• They have a time/completion element. "Earn my teaching certificate" isn't a strong goal. Why? What if it took a person 40 years to do so? A much better goal would be this: "Earn my teaching certificate in four years." The time element gives focus and a sense of urgency to the goal.

• They are tough but doable. Easy-to-obtain goals, such as getting out of bed in the morning, offer little more than a pat-on-the-back. Goals that are too difficult, on the other hand, usually lead to frustration or a sense of being overwhelmed or inadequate. The best goals are what I call "stretch" goals: they can be accomplished, but only when a person pushes him or herself to achieve them.

I recommend creating different goals for the various parts of your life. These "life areas" usually include career, family, spiritual, and personal. You can, of course, create your own.

In addition, some goals should be short-term, with a desired outcome less than a year away, while others should be long-term goals, with an accomplishment date two or five or even ten years in the future.

Examples:

Long-term goal of a 20-year-old: Earn my teaching certificate by my 25th birthday.

Short-term goal of the same 20-year-old: Complete sophomore year of college with a GPA of at least 3.2.

A compelling future vision for your life, combined with specific goals, will offer a target, a destination. How to move forward to reach the target is the subject of the next section.

Moving Toward Your Goals

As I've said, a good attitude is not enough; a person must also take action. Likewise, having a vision of a desirable future is only a beginning; a person must take steps to realize that future. There are four areas I stress when helping others to achieve their goals: time management, combating negative thoughts, developing confidence, and staying committed.

Time Management

The technological advances of the past 30 years, and in particular the last four or five, have made communicating easier. Voicemail, e-mail, wireless communications, personal digital assistants (PDA's), laptop computers, beepers, pagers and the like all have been incorporated into almost everyone's life. In theory, we can do more . . . but even with all of these advances, one important thing hasn't changed: there are still only 24 hours in a day!

Because time is limited, and because we are focused on achieving numerous goals, it has never been more important than now to manage time. Use the following tips and suggestions to manage your time more effectively:

• Develop and use a time-management system. This can be fancy or informal; the key, of course, is to use what works for you. Many pledge allegiance to formal day-planners they carry everywhere. Some have every piece of information they need, or may need, on their computer. Others use something as simple as a calendar adorned with sticky notes. The key is to develop a system you know and trust, and use it!

• Prioritize. If the three most important factors in real estate are location, location, and location, the three most important elements of good time management are prioritize, prioritize, and prioritize. It's tempting to believe you're accomplishing something when you do simple tasks, such as sorting through mail or reviewing magazine articles in your field. But these are "nice to do" activities; they must never distract you from working on goal-achieving tasks.

• Know your body. Everyone during a day has "up" times when he/she feels especially energetic and positive, and also "down" times when concentration and confidence sag. I have colleagues who do their best thinking and preparing very early in the morning, and I also know several people who are "night owls," who really don't get the creative juices flowing until 11:00 p.m. or later. Regardless of when your "up" time is, do your most demanding tasks then, and save the "down" times to do less-structured things, such as sorting mail, answering e-mail, or planning for the next day.

• Learn to say "no." Granted, this is difficult, especially if the request is from a co-worker, family member, or person asking for help with a worthy cause. But those who practice a "less is more" philosophy usually realize that having fewer projects and commitments leads to greater joy and fulfillment on the projects they do tackle.

• Review your goals regularly. This helps keep you "on purpose." Difficult decisions become much easier to make when you review your goals and make your decisions accordingly.

Learning how to best use your time will help you stay focused, even when negative thoughts emerge.

Combating Negative Thoughts

I have a secret to share with you: successful people still experience negative thoughts and fears. In fact, they do so regularly, even when they are at the "top of their game." Why? I believe it's because there is so much negativity in the world today, which seeps, consciously and unconsciously, into our minds.

The successful among us, however, overcome their negative thoughts on a daily basis. They avoid becoming paralyzed by the negativity and fears and, instead, use these as springboards to continue working toward the accomplishments they want to achieve.

For my clients and workshop participants, I offer a simple two-step way to combat negative thinking:

1. Restrain from overreacting to the negative event, person, or influence. Admittedly, this is not easy, but it is a skill that can be learned and certainly worth the effort.

2. Reframe the situation, thought, or event to a manageable situation that may even have a positive outcome.

Here is an example of this in action:

Situation: Asked to fill in for the soloist at a concert.

Negativity: A thought such as, I can't possibly sing a solo with my limited experience.

Restrain from: Even more negative thoughts, such as "The concert hall will be packed with people, and I'll fail and then look like a fool."

Reframe: Instead, think of thoughts such as "This is the opportunity I've been practicing for my whole life!" or "Even if things don't go perfectly, I will have helped out." or "Tonight could be wonderful and I have to start sometime."

As you can see, being confident is closely tied to the idea of combating negative thoughts.

Going with Confidence

I've seen so many people possess the physical and mental abilities to achieve great things in life . . . but they lack one thing: the self-confidence to pursue their dreams. A positive attitude will only do so much for the person lacking confidence.

The following are ways to develop and use confidence:

• Build on past successes. When faced with a difficult or trying situation, think back to a time when you faced a similar problem with positive results. Focus on what you did, the self-talk ideas and images you fed your brain, even the way you talked or acted.

• If you don't have a past success in a particular area, visualize one. If you are preparing to . . . make a speech? write a novel? climb a mountain? Visualize it. Doing anything for the first time is often difficult. But you can watch others do something similar, or read about what others have done and then create a "mental movie" with you succeeding. Make your "mental movies" as colorful and specific as possible: look at the jags on the rocks as you climb higher, listen to the wind whistling through your ears, feel the sun on your arms and legs!

• Expect to win. Confidence comes from within you. Hence, you can "program" your mind with as many positive thoughts as possible. By prepping your mind and focusing on what it is you want to achieve, you will go a long way toward blocking negative thoughts and feelings.

When the participants in the Olympics are preparing for their events, no one thinks, "I can't do this!" Their confidence level has to be as well developed as their athletic skills. They approach the event thinking about the thousands of times they practiced for this moment, and with excitement, skill, and confidence, they show the world how they made it to the top in their field. Anyone who can go as far as the Olympics is a champion. It is important to live your life like a champion!

All of the elements that I have talked about so far will be useless, however, if a person lacks commitment.

Staying Committed

Creating a compelling future complete with specific goals, being able to overcome negative thoughts, and moving forward with confidence are not enough: the person who wants to accomplish the most in life must remain committed,

— no matter how long success takes;

— no matter what obstacles or roadblocks lie in the path;

— no matter that others say, "It can't be done."

Commitment is simply the idea of never giving up. It's vital to achieving what you want to achieve in life. In his book *Over the Top,* noted motivational speaker and coach Zig Ziglar says, "Most people who fail in their dream fail not from lack of ability but from lack of commitment."

To reinforce and strengthen your commitment, focus on the following:

• Reaffirm your commitment every day. Use positive self-talk or affirmations, such as "I will accomplish my goals," and specifically name them. "Today I will continue my quest to become a teacher, a writer, a speaker . . ." or what it is you plan to achieve.

• Limit outside distractions. Everyone needs variety and new learning experiences in life. But allowing "non-essential" hobbies, activities, or pastimes to get in the way of our primary goals and desires hinders our commitment and accomplishments.

• When roadblocks happen, focus on the future. When a star athlete becomes injured, does he or she immediately retire? Of course not: most know that the setback is temporary and work all that much harder to come back. Likewise, each of us will experience delays and setbacks, such as illnesses, a new job or home, or having to assist a friend or relative. These hurdles are not signs to stop permanently; they are obstacles to be cleared so that you can continue your journey.

In my book and in my course on the importance of attitude, I tell the story of professional cyclist Lance Armstrong, who faced enormous physical challenges and overcame them. At one point he was one of the top 15 or 20 cyclists in the world and destined, many said, to win the world's premier bicycle race, the Tour de France. But in 1996 Lance was diagnosed with an advanced case of testicular cancer, one that had spread so much that the doctors told Lance he had a 50-50 chance of surviving and that if he did survive, his career as a professional cyclist would probably be over.

But Lance persevered, battling the cancer with operations and chemotherapy. When he recovered sufficiently, he began riding again. Three years later, in 1999, he became the second American to ever win the coveted Tour de France, and his smile as he rode to victory was as wide as the Champs de Elysees.

Lance Armstrong did not let an obstacle, even one which was life-threatening, stop his dreams of cycling glory. When a person is only interested in something, they pursue it only when convenient. The committed person, however, continues toward the goal no matter what obstacles, temporary setbacks, or roadblocks pop up along the journey.

Summary

There are two critical elements to taking action to accomplish a goal or desired outcome:

1. A person must understand and know the goals that he/she wants to accomplish. (What)

2. A person must begin and then follow through. (How)

As former television journalist Walter Cronkite once said, "I can't image a person becoming a success who doesn't give this game of life everything he's got."

The value, power, and impact of any life is not determined by events but our response to those events. A healthy response includes the appropriate action. Combine your positive attitude with a healthy dose of action, and you'll be well on your way to accomplishing far more than you ever expected. Enjoy the journey!

ABOUT
MARY KAY KURZWEG

*M*ary Kay Kurzweg speaks internationally on the different factors that
motivate us and how we can capitalize on these to become more
effective leaders, productive participants and more understanding participants in our relationships. In a light and entertaining manner, Mary Kay
shows people how to make a difference through trust, leadership and communication. Her clients include Edison Electric Institute in Washington,
D.C., Landmark Incentive Marketing in Bangkok, the National Institutes of
Health in Washington, D.C., the Apache Reservation in White Mountain,
AZ, and many other business, education and government organizations.

Contact Information:
Mary Kay Kurzweg
MMK & Co.
215 Stella Street
Metairie, LA 70005
phone (800) 493-2983 or (504) 833-0277
fax: (504) 835-7733
e-mail: MKKurzweg@aol.com
web: www.CallMaryKay.com

LIFE IS AN OPPORTUNITY AND BALANCE IS A CHOICE:

The Gentle Art of Creating "Life Balance" Blending Your Personal and Professional Worlds

by Valla Dana Fotiades, M.Ed.

Every summer I have the choice and opportunity to spend a little time, usually about one glorious week, at my childhood cottage. I take off my watch when I arrive and never put it back on until moments before I leave. Great things happen! It's a wonderful window of time to relish being with my family and my children *and* to, momentarily, be a kid again. We canoe, snorkel, swim, fish, call the loons, paint, carve, perhaps take a special class, and sometimes even participate in the lake's annual family regatta and win a ribbon for our efforts. Accomplishment? Life Balance!

We are a beautiful mosaic of the varied and special experiences we have had in life. We develop our own code of values about what is true and what is important in life from people who have influenced us, inspired us, and encouraged us to do more than we may have ever dreamed possible. We accomplish many things in a multitude of areas in our life. Looking at accomplishment, I truly believe we need to create our own definition of what that means for us individually.

With that in mind, I present to you some thoughts about the fine art of blending your professional and personal lives to balance your life and arrive at your own definition of accomplishment.

My dad, Hop, chose to pursue a career that he absolutely loved. This was a gift to me as a life lesson on accomplishment. He didn't make a zillion dollars as a college professor and a coach, but he did have a wonderfully fulfilling career. Hop was always learning in order to be able to teach new programs that were adopted in his physical education department. Thousands of students were touched through his 30-plus years as a coach at Eastern Illinois University. Recently, at a reunion planned by one of his former wrestlers, Hop learned that many of his students, and now even their sons, had become wrestling coaches because of his positive influence and enthusiasm. That is an accomplishment: Making a difference in the lives of generations to come.

So you see, from my dad, I learned to: 1) pursue a career you love; 2) constantly pursue learning; 3) do something to make a difference in the lives of others and have fun while you are doing it!

My mother, Evy, who is another one of my greatest supporters, is also a life-long learner and teacher. She went back to college when I started the first grade. Evy would take one course at a time. When she finally marched down that aisle in her cap and gown — she was 40! (I was six when she started and 15 when she finished.) It is never too late to do something you want to do. She went on to get two masters degrees after that. She had been at almost every special event in my life; it was her priority to be there for her children.

I learned from my mother: 1) patience is essential to finally achieving what you want; 2) it is never too late to try something new; 3) be true to what is important for you, and stick to it in order to balance your life priorities.

What kinds of life lessons have you learned along the way that have guided your life focus? What are you imparting as life lessons to people in your life?

Remember how I mentioned we learn from others along the path of life? Well, besides those wonderful life lessons I gathered from my folks, I had people who have, often unbeknownst to them, directed the focus in my life.

Following are seven questions that have provided a guide for my focus as I continually work to accomplish my goals in life. I share them with you for "thought food."

1) *What are you leaving as a lasting legacy? For your family? In your workplace? In the world we live in?*

Leave a Lasting Legacy was the theme of the National Speakers Association under the presidential leadership of Glenna Salsbury. That theme inspired me to think a lot about, *"How am leaving this world a better place because I have had the privilege to open my eyes today?"*

My legacy is opening pathways of inspiration for others. How do I accomplish or try to accomplish this? There are many answers. First, as a mother, I have worked on imparting to my children the importance of sharing sincere compliments and of trying to make the people with whom we interact each day feel glad that we crossed their path. If each of us concentrated on doing this each day, it could have a powerful effect on the world. *Example*: When a colleague of mine, who is a highly successful businessman and someone I greatly respect, turned to me while we were working on a project together and said, "You work smart." You can be sure that his compliment has echoed many times in my ears over the years.

You might be saying to yourself, "Well, Valla, how many people can that really affect?" Let me share what I call the PPS Principle. PPS stands for the "Privilege and the Power of the Stage." As Shakespeare wrote, "We are all actors on the stage." YOU are on stage 24 hours a day as a human being. You may be at work, at home, at the post office, at the grocery store, playing tennis, volunteering somewhere, or just anywhere! You have the privilege to share kind thoughts, words, and deeds everywhere you venture. You have the power to inspire others to be better, to try something new, to grow.

Your words could be the inspiring echo people hear in their mind that encourages them to go on because you believed in them when they didn't yet see what they might be capable of accomplishing. In numbers, it works like this. Say you take on as a challenge to affect one person each day in a positive way for the next year (365 days). In one year you will have affected 365 people. If each of those folks you positively affect does something positive (you bet, it is a contagious thing to do!), in one more year of 365 people x 365 days of sharing good thoughts and encouraging words and doing kind deeds, 133,956 will be affected. Follow this through for one more year in which 133,956 people are doing just one positive act each day and look! — over a three-year-period you will have affected and brightened the lives of 48, 983,940 people. You can create an incredible lasting legacy.

$$
\begin{array}{r}
365 \\
\underline{\times 1} \\
365 \\
\underline{\times 365} \\
133{,}956 \\
\underline{\times 365} \\
\mathbf{48{,}983{,}940}
\end{array}
$$

           365
            x1
           365 people positively affected in one year
          x365
    133,956 people positively affected in two years
         x365
48,983,940 *people positively affected in three years*

Mark Twain once said, "The really great make you feel that you, too, can somehow be great." Each day, work on seeing what is "right" with others and giving them sincere compliments. Think of what each of us could do for our world by focusing on encouraging, inspiring, or just being kind to two or three people per day. What is realistic for you? What do you think you might be able to accomplish each day? A really good idea is to give yourself sincere compliments on the little things done "right" each day. You will be surprised how much more energy you feel when you do this with regularity.

2) *How would you like to be remembered?*

Can you put your answer in a sentence or two? Maybe you could think of 5-7 descriptive words that could describe how you would like to be remembered.

Do you think you could ask 3-5 of your closest friends to give you this answer? It is a tough question. In my experience trying to answer this, it has made me more thoughtful in all the facets of my life — at home, at work, at play.

What an accomplishment to figure this answer out early in life. It could be very instrumental in helping you focus on your daily behavior. I really hope that when I am gone, people will remember me by saying, "She inspired people to pursue their dreams. She helped people communicate more effectively. She brightened the lives of the people she touched. She was fun, knowledgeable, creative, humorous, and a delight to be around."

Every day we have a choice and an opportunity to be. What kind of magic will you accomplish when you add in to your life the goal of achieving how you want to be remembered?

3) *What are your top 10-12 priorities in life?*

I am curious. Did health hit the top of your list? If you have ever had someone in your life deal with a chronic disease or terminal illness, my guess is health would hit #1 on your chart!

My mom is a cancer survivor. My mother-in-law survived cancer and quadruple by-pass surgery. My husband deals daily with a disease that causes him to be in chronic pain. When people are dealing with these kinds of situations, priorities in life shift.

When my mom was diagnosed, I realized very quickly that some people do not have the privilege to wake up in the morning. She said, "All the money in the world, unfortunately, cannot buy your health back for you."

Well, it once again reinforced in my life to make time for the business of living each day to the fullest. Grasp the specialness of momentary "doses of daily delight" as Paul Pearsall speaks about in his book, *The Pleasure Prescription: To Love, to Work, to Play — Life in the Balance*.

As for accomplishment, I do believe we redefine what accomplishment is to us when we meet these types of life experiences and actively seek more balance in our lives. The definition of accomplishment may then change to become: watching a sunset with the people in your life who mean a lot to you, taking a day or two or maybe a few hours from one's busy schedule to log in some "kick-back" time to be with someone special, spending some extra time in your garden, or maybe just relaxing and reading a book for the fun of it.

As you have probably guessed, my top priority is health. Up there right along side it would be my family, my spirituality, my desire to help and inspire others find their potential, my mission to make someone else's day a bit better because I passed their way, and my determination to cultivate my talents to excel in my professional career as a speaker, author, TV host, and adjunct professor. I must get regular exercise, and walking and working in my garden are both extremely important in my regular routine. And I make time to pursue learning for business and pleasure — reading, classes, lectures, conferences.

If you take time to really think about what your top priorities are and if you knew that you had a limited time left here, what would you choose to do differently? What would you do more of or start doing?

On many occasions I have heard people who have been extremely successful, if defined and measured by money and recognition factors, who have shared from their heart that, if they could change anything in their life, they would have spent more time with their family.

It's a delicate balance and the choices are sometimes difficult to make, but if you keep your priorities straight and follow your heart, my guess is you will choose what is right for you at the right time.

4) *Do you love what you do?*

Remember? This is what I learned from my dad even though I did not realize it at that time. It is a great accomplishment to love what you do. My dad's father was a high-powered businessman who was very desirous of making a lot of money. And you know what? He did. He could never understand my father's lack (in Grandpa's eyes) of motivation to make a huge salary. Well, my dad was a professor, a coach and a really fun dad. He was around a lot. Every weekend he would take us to the gym to play on the trampoline and gymnastic equipment and then go swimming. Accomplishments? Not based on $$$ signs, but on living a life that was full of learning, fun, play, healthy competition, and a good dose of balance.

Some people ask me, "How do you manage to do all the things that you do?" My answer is simple. I am in charge of my schedule. I am employed as a consultant by Fallon Healthcare System to host a TV show called *For Your Health*. As I write this, we have just launched our sixth season. I love meeting the guests, pre-interviewing them, and creating our script outline. And it's fun to make it all happen on TV. We share information that is extremely practical, and we make a difference in the lives of the people we touch. That is accomplishment to me.

My second job is teaching at Quinsigamond Community College, where I teach one Speech Communications class each semester. With my background as a professional speaker and having attended numerous meetings, conventions, conferences and coaching sessions, I wanted to share my expertise with people who could benefit by practicing the many techniques I have learned over the years. The exciting part is how students see/feel/hear the connections and how they directly apply to their everyday life. It is leaving a lasting legacy for them to share and making a difference for life. Yes, that is also accomplishment in my eyes.

When my daughter, Dana, who is now twelve was in preschool, my dentist asked me if I would like to work for her. She explained that it would be only one day a week. If I needed to be home with a sick child or be away on a vacation, it would be fine. Sounded flexible. I had done office work many times as I was going through school, so I agreed. The day I quit that job was the morning after I finished reading a chapter in a book called, *Living With Joy*. You see, the book said something like, "When you think of your work, you should have good, joyful thoughts. If you are dreading going in to work, you are doing damage to your spirit." A huge relief came over me when I gave notice that morning. It released me to pursue the kind of work that fuels my spirit with joy and enthusiasm, and that is being a professional speaker, my third job.

Think about your own situation. Do you love what you do? If not, what kinds of steps can you take to help a new and better work situation evolve? Sometimes it may require going back to school for some new training. One of my good friends ended up in a divorce when she had two preschoolers. She went back to school part-time, while holding down two jobs to pay the bills. She pursued her long-sought-after dream to be a travel agent. Guess what? She did it! It took awhile. Patience was definitely a virtue. She has won several trips to faraway places that she always dreamed of visiting. Do what you love to do, and your work becomes a joyful experience. Loving what you do is a marvelous way to keep yourself refreshed with life.

Oh, yes, and then there are my "other jobs"! Are you a volunteer for any group, organization, association that you feel strongly about? From experience, I can tell you money cannot buy the experience we gain from giving out of the true spirit of service. Do the things you love to do because they come easily to you. You may be asked by others to do some things that allow you to challenge yourself to grow because they know you can do what you do not yet realize.

As a past president of the New England Speakers Association, I have had multiple opportunities to work with a variety of people in our National Speakers Association. Those experiences would not have opened up for me if I had not been drawn in to give in the spirit of service at the local level. As a matter of fact, this book chapter opportunity came my way because of a colleague, Deborah Dahm, another author in this book. Deborah has asked me to be on her leadership team for fun events at our national conventions over the last several years. Due to my experience of having worked with her, I was able to pass along her name when the National Speakers Association was looking to fill a regional leadership position.

Because I had worked with her, I knew her eye for detail and excellent leadership and communication skills would be an asset to the team.

Oftentimes, I have opened pathways for my colleagues to speak on stage at the national level, and they say, "How can I ever repay you?" My response is always, "Do something kind, encouraging, pathway-opening for someone else because I am blessed to have a whole lot of people opening pathways for me."

Volunteer for something you strongly believe in. You will grow personally and professionally and have fun while you are doing it.

5) What truly inspires you, fills your spirit with joy, makes you feel wonderfully excited about each day and ecstatic that you woke up this morning? Survey yourself.

I remember a colleague asking me, back in the mid-80s, to write down what I wanted to be doing in 10 years. I found that paper about three years ago while I was going through some files. This is what I had said: "I wanted to complete my Masters degree (which happened one class at a time while having two young children). I wanted to be speaking to large audiences and sharing information that would help them lead happier, more fulfilling, healthier lives." WOW! What a fascinating find! It is exactly what I am doing.

Lesson for me! Write down your visions, your dreams, your hopes, and somehow your body's energy starts helping you work toward these goals. I am not quite sure how it works, but I do know that it does. Try it! Let me know how it works for you.

6) *How do you start your day?*

Do you, upon awakening each morning, take a moment to breathe deeply? Smile? Go over, in your mind, all the things that are "right" with your life? Try it! It has a way of starting off your day in an immune-system-boosting way.

7) *Are you creating time for "Life Balance" with your professional and personal roles?*

a) Create your priority list. Follow through.

b) Mark important dates. Keep them free.

Example: Mark family birthdays, celebrations, athletic meets, holidays, vacations. I have heard of people who were unable to make their children's graduations because of business. You are in charge. Take care of the business of life first.

c) Make dates with the significant people in your life.

Example: My neighbors have four children. The daddy is a trouble-shooter for an elevator company and often "on-call" on the weekend. He makes it a ritual to take a different child with him on-call. It is a special time for both.

Example: If you find it hard to get a chance to just "talk" with your significant other, plan a special time each day or week to spend time alone. You might take a walk or a ride (cell phones turned off!) just to stay in touch.

Example: Three of my friends and I started a reading circle a few years ago. We read/study a book and then discuss the ideas. We meet once every 4-6 weeks for about 3-4 hours. It has become something that we all look forward to. In this very busy world of ours, it is rare to block off a significant amount of time to discuss values, beliefs, and dreams. Highly recommended.

d) Fuel your creative juices.

Example: Read books that inspire you. Ask someone you know, "What is the best thing you have read lately?" It is fun and interesting to hear their response.

Example: Take a class. Learn something new. Last year when we moved into our own house, my husband and son took a home mainte-nance class together. We have been "doing things" on the house ever since and still have many hours of house adventure left.

Maybe you want to take a painting, public speaking, sailing or golf class. Who knows? Think about it and then take action and sign up. It may work like a form of meditative stress reduction as it does for me, or it could evolve into a fun and financially profitable career!

In the fall of 1991, I took a class on TV production. On January 13, 1992, I launched my first TV show called *"Networking Women."* After 10 shows, my husband's idea to rename the show seemed a great one because the information shared was designed to inform, educate, enter-tain, and motivate. This show later became *"Valla & Company."* We taped shows for three-and-a-half years.

It was because of this Cable Access TV experience that I was hired by Fallon Healthcare System as a TV Host. So you see, you never quite know where and how your former accomplishments may thrust you to new levels of accomplishment.

I hope these seven questions help you along your path to accom-plishment in your life. Which ideas will you use and which ones will you share with others?

Best of luck in creating "Life Balance" in your professional and personal life.

ABOUT
VALLA DANA FOTIADES, M.ED.

*V*alla Dana Fotiades is an energizer, consultant, author, television host and speaker. She works with individuals and organizations who want to learn fresh techniques for energizing and better skills for communicating. The results are people who are more balanced, enthusiastic and productive. Clients from different industries offer comments such as, "Great ideas that are practical, inexpensive and applicable . . . They work! . . . It gave me redirection in my life! . . . A joyous learning experience!" Valla is host of the television show, "For Your Health." She's co-author of the book, "Teaching & Joy." She's an adjunct professor and a past president of the New England Speakers Association.

Contact Information:
Valla Dana Fotiades
Energize Your Life!
P.O.Box 812 West Side Station
Worchester, MA 01602-0812
phone: (508) 799-9860
fax: (508) 755-3659
e-mail: VallaDana@cs.com

LEADERSHIP – THE HEART OF ORGANIZATIONAL ACCOMPLISHMENT

by Steve Lishansky

To understand leadership, the driving force of accomplishment in organizations, it is also necessary to understand some of the key elements that determine the levels of accomplishment in the personal and interpersonal domains. Organizations, large and small, are nothing other than collections of individuals working together for the purpose of producing exponentially greater results than any individual alone could produce. By discovering the forces that determine how an individual or a relationship will maximize its potential, we unlock some of the underlying keys to understanding leadership and organizational success.

Accomplishment Element #1: Individual Fulfillment

The fundamental building blocks of every organization or team are the individuals that constitute that group. One of the greatest mistakes of under-performing organizations is that they are redefining processes, installing new systems or even seeking to improve communications without taking into account the essential element that is most important — the people.

General Norman Schwartzkopf, the celebrated leader of the allied forces in the Persian Gulf War with Iraq, said this was a constant issue in the Army. He tells the story of taking a talented, but rigid and overbearing captain for a lesson in leadership. This captain equated giving orders with leading. Schwartzkopf knew from years of experience that you absolutely cannot treat people like things. He had the captain stand in front of one of the Army's largest and most powerful new tanks, and told him to command the tank. As he delivered his crisp orders to the tank, the results were predictable — nothing happened. The captain learned the most fundamental law of leadership: you lead people; you do not lead things.

Without the people, nothing happens. In the most automated plants and computerized processes we can imagine, people are behind the conceptualization, the development, and the implementation. When something goes wrong, it is people who repair our automated wonders. Disregard the people and their importance in making things happen, and you are destined for difficulty.

This leads to one of the core questions any great leader must learn to answer: What moves individuals to be their best and contribute their greatest assets in their life and in their endeavors? We all know people, both famous and unknown, who seem to have the extra energy, the greater clarity, and the superior results indicative of the happy and "on purpose" individual. What do they have in greater abundance than the average person?

I suggest that one of the substantive differences between the average and the most successful lies in the elements of fulfillment that an individual is able to tap. The most powerful touchstones of individual fulfillment include a strong sense of identity, clarity of purpose, and the ability to articulate and live by one's highest values. Starting here, the successful individual is much more able to manifest his or her empowering beliefs (versus those energy-sucking, disempowering beliefs), establish personal goals in harmony with their purpose and values, and choose actions that are congruent and aligned with who they really are. The results: greater ease and more powerful results that do, in fact, add up to a life of fulfillment.

The wise leader takes into account these dramatically powerful elements for every individual when considering how to build organizational success and accomplishment. Otherwise, we risk falling through one of the "trap doors" that seem to steal energy, effort, and results from our organizations.

I have to make an important note about fulfillment at this point, based upon my experiences with many high-powered and motivated individuals. Many people, especially those who have a strong drive towards goals but who have not tasted the level of fulfillment they really want, are afraid that a high level of fulfillment will "sap" their drive or determination. Nothing could be further from the truth.

If you value the feelings of creativity, freedom, contribution, vitality, love, connection with others, or any of the other high-level values many top performers hold as important, will having the taste of these satiate you or inspire you to want to keep these feelings alive? These are the fuel of human excellence, commitment, and performance, as well as an important element of the foundations of fulfillment. Missing these is the bigger challenge. Many people have clear goals, but not clear vision, values, or purpose. Achieving goals without a clear sense of how they align with your purpose, fulfill your vision, or match your values often leads to the cynical question too many outwardly "successful" people are asking themselves: Is this all there is?

Too many individuals today struggle with stress, are overwhelmed and frustrated in their professional and personal lives. The person who is "on purpose," living their values and following their vision will almost always be more productive, happy, clear thinking, objective, and ready to do anything that is aligned with his or her vision, values and purpose — and do it with energy, passion, and determination. They are the individuals who have a zest for life, an appetite for challenging work, and a desire to contribute in meaningful ways. Every organization needs these fulfillment-driven people for their willingness to do more than you could ever ask them to do, to create new and more productive ways of accomplishing essential tasks, and to provide a contagious sense of contribution, excitement, and innovation.

Accomplishment Element #2: Interpersonal Productivity

Let's assume you have individuals with a high level of drive towards fulfillment in your organization. Certainly this is an excellent start. Now we can examine the next step in the progression towards outstanding leadership and organizational accomplishment — the need for greater productivity in the way our people interact and work together.

A famous consultant once said: "After working in dozens of top organizations, it never fails to amaze me how you can take intelligent men and women, put them in a room, and they come out with a decision only an idiot could make." What is it that allows our great individual talents to lose their edge and ability to be productive when asked to collaborate with other talented people?

The very word productivity makes us ask whether or not we are getting the kind and level of results we seek from the working together that we do. All of us have seen teams and organizations that, working together, seem to do the amazing, the impossible, and even the miraculous. We have also seen those groups of highly talented, experienced, and intelligent people who cannot seem to get out of their own way and produce even modest results.

I suggest that the issue of productivity is determined by our ability — or inability — to influence and build relationships with other people. This essential and fundamental interpersonal skill is at the heart of our ability to produce outstanding results by substantially increasing our productivity.

We often find those who cannot work well together being sent to courses on listening and communications, and other so-called "soft skills" courses. "Soft skills" is very often being used as a thinly veiled pejorative in my experience. I counter with this about the ability to influence and build relationships: these skills are to business success what software is to effective computing. Your computer will not work without software, and your business will not function, much less at a high level, without these influence and relationship-building skills.

I will say this about listening and communicating as the focus of training or attention: they are not what is ultimately most important. At Success Dynamics we have coined these phrases to make sure our clients know what to focus upon:

"Listening is not what is really important — understanding is."

"Communicating is not what is really important — influencing is."

Too many times we get fixated upon the means, or the vehicles we are using, to take us someplace. Then we forget where we are really going. Is listening really the essential result — or is it the way to get what we really need and want: the ability to understand another person? Is communicating what we are really aiming for and desiring, or do we really seek the ability to influence and move others? The biggest problem with getting stuck in our vehicles is that we forget where we are going, and then get frustrated that the vehicle is not taking us to a great destination. We blame the vehicle for failing to deliver us to a place we can only vaguely describe, but expect to arrive at. As with navigating anywhere, you will not arrive at your destination if you do not know where your destination really is.

We must distinguish between understanding what someone's words mean and the meaning that a person has created for his or her words. Without elaborating on our Success Dynamics influence model in detail, we can say that failure to understand another person is a precursor to failure to be able to influence him or her. Failure to influence or move another person is consistent with the inability to create a high-value relationship with that person. Lacking either the ability to influence or the basis for a high-value relationship with another person is almost certain to result in a seriously deficient ability to work together well, much less be productive.

On the other hand, the cycle of success in productivity is not difficult to build and is absolutely essential for long-term leadership results and accomplishment. In simple terms, by having rapport with others, seeking to understand what is really important to them, clarifying what actions would support their getting what is most important to them, and then acting upon your mutual commitments, you have the basis for a high-value relationship. People who can understand another's points of view and interact with regard for producing high-value outcomes together, are in a position to create a level of influence and relationship that is a hallmark of high performance groups. Their efficiency as well as effectiveness is often greater, not by degrees, but by magnitudes, over their poorly-equipped-to-communicate brethren.

Accomplishment Element #3: Organizational Leadership

The issues of individual fulfillment and interpersonal productivity are key underpinnings of any great organization. No leader intent upon any serious level of accomplishment can ignore the personal satisfaction of individuals in his or her company, nor can he or she fail to be concerned about the level of effective interaction of their people. Yet even these alone may not yield the exceptional accomplishment you see around the great leaders.

Leadership is often spoken about in terms that remind me of the story of the four blind men and the elephant. Each blind man was led to a part of the elephant but asked to describe the entire elephant. The one holding the elephant's tail proclaimed: "The elephant is like a rope." The blind individual holding the elephant's ear protested: "No, no. The elephant is like a huge tobacco leaf." The third man was touching the elephant's body and said: "The elephant is like a big wall." The fourth blind man, holding the elephant's leg, decided: "The elephant is really like a tree trunk."

On the one hand, they were all accurate in their analogies. On the other hand, we do not really know very much about the nature of the elephant or what it is really like. Most of the literature about leadership is like that — we hear numerous anecdotes about the point of contact the writer has with leadership, but do not necessary understand the phenomenon or nature of leadership. This is one of the reasons that leadership seems somewhat mystical or mystifying — we do not know what to look at or look for to truly understand leadership and its critical role in organizational accomplishment.

We do recognize great leadership when we see it manifested in the accomplishment of companies, organizations, or countries. We see Steve Jobs of the 1990's (certainly not to be confused with the Steve Jobs of the 1970's and 1980's) rescuing Apple Computer from a final death march everyone else thought it would never recover from. Not only did it recover, it rewrote the rules and captured the imagination of the marketplace with its best selling iMacs. In less than two years, Apple's stock exploded more than six-fold.

Jack Welsh is often cited as the executive with the golden touch. Taking over GE in 1981, when it was a well-established but perhaps stodgy industrial powerhouse, he lead the expansion of its stock value from $6 billion dollars to over $300 billion dollars. He shed many businesses, but he also developed GE into the leader in many fields, including his biggest profit engine — GE Capital.

Charles Schwab led his company to the head of the pack in his chosen field not once but twice. As the first giant of the discount stock brokerage business, Schwab helped create today's financial revolution. However, after a while he started to find his market share and profitability sliding. In the manner of a truly great leader, he and his team reinvented themselves and their company a second time, establishing themselves as the leader in the new field of on-line stock trading.

Bernard Ebbers started a little telephone company in Mississippi in the 1980's. A decade later he is the CEO of the second-largest telecommunications company in the United States, MCI-WorldCom. His leadership has been instrumental in not just acquiring some of the biggest and best names in the business, but also in redefining the entire industry. To sustain his growth at such an astounding pace, he has successfully built an exceptional team of telecom experts and has them working together with speed, focus, and effectiveness.

There are many more examples in our time of great leaders. Unfortunately, there are even more examples of poor leadership. What makes the difference, a difference that often affects the lives and families of tens or hundreds of thousands of people? Why do the luminaries cited above accomplish so much, while so many others fail or accomplish so little relative to their expected potential?

To address what leadership is and does, let us first ask what it is not. I often ask my audiences and clients one of our core questions on leadership: What is the opposite of leadership? You would be surprised at the range of responses: management, thinking too much, not making decisions, not taking responsibility, and so on. Each of these may possess a modicum of truth, but when asked to explain why one of these is the opposite of leadership, most people cannot come up with a coherent rationale. To me, this points up the limitations in our thinking about the topic. If we cannot define what something is, we probably cannot competently define what it is not.

At Success Dynamics we have thought long and hard about this question before crafting our answer. For us, the opposite of leadership is *reaction*. Our thinking goes like this: The primary focus of reaction is the past. Reaction is about accommodating the past and trying to make it into the present.

The primary focus of leadership is the future. Leadership is about starting with the present and designing and navigating towards a compelling future. Given this strong focus in the future, we see the opposite of leadership as reaction. Furthermore, if you were to look at organizations that have poor leadership, you will soon begin describing the environment as highly reactive, another confirmation for us that where leadership fails, reaction takes over.

What Are the Characteristics of a Highly Accomplished Organization?

To characterize a highly accomplished organization in the simplest terms possible, it is highly productive, highly profitable, and highly fulfilled, the key characteristics of productivity and fulfillment we have discussed in relation to interpersonal and individual accomplishment. The key organizational measure, profitability, means far more than dollars on the bottom line, although that must be a key criterion. In terms of organizational accomplishments, profitability also includes the following results at the end of a year, relative to where they were at the beginning of the year:

- Your team is more inspired, skilled and capable.
- You have greater clarity of vision and stronger alignment throughout your organization.
- You have greater clarity, commitment, and capability to achieve your objectives.
- There is more and better innovation happening throughout your organization.
- Your marketplace is better developed and more welcoming of your products and services.
- Your customer relationships are better and more valuable.
- You are better positioned in the market to grow and prosper.

These are all results that a strong and accomplished leader must produce in his or her company or group. I think that you can begin to see how the fulfillment and drive of highly engaged individuals, who are working together with strong influence and relationship-building skills, are essential to the level of accomplishment we are pointing to in the bullet points above. A leader has the ultimate responsibility for creating this kind of environment and these kinds of results.

What is it that the talented, skilled, and committed leader needs to know and do to make sure that all of this comes to fruition?

The Essential Elements of Leadership

When I talk about the essential elements of leadership, I aim to illuminate universal principles that apply to leadership in all situations and circumstances. Rather than touching a part of leadership, let us explore the very essence of what is universal about outstanding leadership. What I propose here are five essential elements that distinguish a great leader. The degree of manifestation of all of these elements determines the level of leadership accomplishment — and organizational results — you can expect to observe.

The five fundamental elements of great leaders and leadership are:

1. Vision — Defining a compelling future vision that stimulates the passion and commitment of associates, management, customers and shareholders.

2. Navigating Alignments — Building and maintaining the harmony of essential processes. These could include alignments of issues such as missions, goals and strategies; the best interests of the customers, associates and the company; and personal, inter-personal and organizational objectives, to name a few.

3. Influence — Leveraging yourself through others with high-impact communications and relationship building skills, that is, creating compelling win-win opportunities in your interactions with others.

4. Being Your Best — Harnessing your greatest assets and talents to make your best decisions, lead your people, and be an example to your organization (the fact is that leaders are always an example to their people of what is acceptable).

5. Bring Out the Best in Your People — Leveraging the skills, capabilities, desires, and best efforts of your personnel through fostering a learning environment, providing coaching and mentoring, and supporting the maximization of their talents, contributions, and results.

Look at your favorite examples of outstanding leaders and organizations and ask yourself: Do they match these essential elements in the leadership model? Every great leader and organization has a powerful vision around which to focus their work and development. Part of the vision Jack Welsh laid out for GE was that they would be either #1 or #2 in their industry, or they would not be part of GE. Steve Jobs, upon regaining control of the dying Apple Computer, declared that they would once again lead the computer industry in design and innovation, at the top end of the market and at the consumer level. Within one year, Apple rolled out the machines that fulfilled his vision, enabling the company to once again begin writing a new chapter for Apple and the whole industry.

Once vision is defined and becomes a driving force in the organization, a great leader begins navigating alignment inside and outside the company, in all critical areas for success. The key is to have a vision so clear that the leadership and organization use it to align their efforts, operations, and results.

In order to keep navigating the alignments, it is vitally important to have the ability to influence people, teams, and even the marketplace. Jack Welsh, even as CEO of a company with hundreds of thousands of employees, says in his biography that he spends a third of his time travelling the world to speak with GE employees and customers. He believes this is one of the most critical aspects of his continuing success — telling everyone at GE who they are, where they are going, and why they are doing what they are doing. These are, in fact, the most critical elements that constitute vision. Jack Welsh makes sure that his vision is understood — and acted upon.

To influence others, you must be an example of your best. As a leader, you must demonstrate your own commitment to your continual growth and development and excellence if you expect others to follow your lead. I am not talking about being perfect. What is impressive is a leader who models what he or she expects, including dealing with his or her weaknesses.

The strongest way to continually strengthen and grow your organization is to constantly bring out the best in your people. From supporting the continuous improvement of your people with an organizational environment that fosters growth and learning, to coaching and mentoring them, to supporting their personal visions, a great leader is increasing profitability in a profound and long-lasting way.

Leadership — the Ultimate Organizational Accomplishment

As you can see, leadership is where the challenges of the entire enterprise must be met. Whether dealing with an individual, an interpersonal or an organization-wide issue, the leader must have the understanding, wherewithal, and skill to address whatever comes up in the context of the elements of great leadership. One of the traits of the finest leaders is their ability to create new leaders. This is the ultimate leverage of outstanding leaders — their ability to multiply themselves, and create new leaders who will also grow to multiply themselves. This multiplication factor is one of the key indicators of the highly successful and accomplished leader and organization.

ABOUT
STEVE LISHANSKY

S teve Lishansky, President of Success Dynamics, is a recognized expert in leadership and executive development. He is known among his clients as the Executive Catalyst for his skill and ability in partnering with them to Turn Their Potential into Results™. Steve provides customized executive coaching, consulting, keynote speeches and learning for top corporate leaders and their organizations. He founded two fast-growth, multi-million dollar businesses and served as the sales and marketing vice president for a third. He is the founder of the Executive Coaching Institute, the leading executive coach training school in the United States.

His clients include leaders from organizations as diverse as Anderson Consulting, Fleet Bank, PricewaterhouseCoopers, EMC, MetLife, American Management Systems, SunAmerica Securities, Oakley, the Federal Aviation Administration and numerous entrepreneurial organizations.

Contact Information:
Steve Lishansky
Success Dynamics
83 Whits End Road
Concord, MA 02482
phone: (978) 369-4525
phone: (888) 669-4753
fax: (978) 369-2324
e-mail: SLishansky@SuccessDynamics.com
web: www.SuccessDynamics.com

RESOURCES

Christina Bergenholtz, M.Ed.
P.O. Box 301
Grafton, MA 01519
✆ (508) 839-5139
fax: (508) 887-9556
e-mail: chrismhb@aol.com

Jan Cannon, Ph.D.
Cannon Business Development
38 Orchard Street
Belmont, MA 02478-3010
✆ (617) 484-5998 or (800) 550-4544
e-mail: Coach@Cannon4Success.com
web: www.Cannon4Success.com

Deborah Dahm
Accredited Seminars and Presentations
3315B Covington Court
Hutchinson, KA 67502
✆ (316) 663-3371
fax: (316) 663-3372
e-mail: DLDahm@midusa.net
web: www.DebListens.com

Valla Dana Fotiades, M.Ed.
Energize Your Life!
P.O. Box 812 West Side Station
Worchester, MA 01602-0812
✆ (508) 799-9860
fax: (508) 755-3659
e-mail: VallaDana@cs.com

Marianne Frederick, MHSA
WorkPlay, Inc.
14 Bridgewood Ave.
Taylors, SC 29687
✆ (864) 268-1541
fax: (864) 268-1541
e-mail: MFredck@aol.com

Valerie Jones, M.B.A.
Quantum Resource Consulting
165 Shady Brooke Walk
Fairburn, GA 30213
✆ (770) 461-9042
fax: (770) 461-9043
e-mail: VYJones@aol.com

Mary Kay Kurzweg
MMK & Co.
215 Stella Street
Metairie, LA 70005
✆ (800) 493-2983
✆ (504) 833-0277
fax: (504) 835-7733
e-mail: MKKurzweg@aol.com
web: www.CallMaryKay.com

Steve Lishansky
Success Dynamics
83 Whits End Road
Concord, MA 02482
✆ (978) 369-4525
✆ (888) 669-4753
fax: (978) 369-2324
e-mail: SLishansky@SuccessDynamics.com
web: www.SuccessDynamics.com

Myra McElhaney
McElhaney & Assoc.
8531 Birch Hollow Drive
Roswell, GA 30076
✆ (770) 664-4553
fax: (770) 752-0817
e-mail: MyraMcElhaney@mindspring.com
web: speakerspages.com/MyraMcElhaney

Snowden McFall
Brightwork Advertising and Training
74 Northeastern Blvd., Unit 20
Nashua, NH 03062
✆ (888) FIREBKS
✆ (603) 882-0600
e-mail: SMcFall@FiredUp-TakeAction-Now.com
web: www.FiredUp-TakeAction-Now.com

Barbara Mintzer
B.A. Mintzer & Associates
4019A Otono Drive
Santa Barbara, CA 93110
✆ (800) 845-3211
✆ (805) 964-7546
fax: (805) 964-9636
e-mail: bmintzer@west.net
web: www.Speaking.com/Mintzer.html

Maureen Murray, M.S.Ed.
Humor Associates
225 Outlook Drive
Pittsburgh, PA 15228
✆ (412) 561-1577
fax: (412) 561-1559
e-mail: MMurrayHA@aol.com

Rick Phillips
Phillips Sales and Staff Development
P.O. Box 29615
New Orleans, LA 70189
✆ (800) 525-PSSD (7773)
e-mail: PSSD@web-net.com
web: www.RickPhillips.com

Carol Pierce, M.Ed.
Success NOW!
P.O. Box 250
Raceland, LA 70394
© (504) 537-5713
© (877) JumpNow
fax: (504) 537-3187
e-mail: Carol@JumpNow.com
web: www.JumpNow.com

Sharyn Scheyd
Sharyn Scheyd, Inc.
P.O. Box 641642
Kenner, LA 70064
© (800) 4-SharYn (474-2796)
e-mail: callSharYn@aol.com
web: www.nolaspeaks.com/SharYn

Dan Thurmon
InfoMedia, Inc.
4805 Lawrenceville Hwy., Suite 116
Lilburn, GA 30047
© (770) 923-3788
e-mail: Dan@DanThurmon.com

Jodi Walker
Success Alliances
9018 Balboa Blvd., PMB #617
Northridge, CA 91325
© (800) 782-1719
fax: (818) 894-4329
e-mail: JodiWalker@aol.com
web: www.JodiWalker.com

Bruce Wilkinson, CSP
Workplace Consultants, Inc.
1799 Stumpf Blvd., Bldg. 3, Suite 6B
Gretna, LA 70056
✆ (504) 368-2994
fax: (504) 368-0993
e-mail: SpeakPoint@aol.com